DOUBLE TAKE

DOUBLE TAKE

A Comparative Look at Photographs

by Richard Whelan

Foreword by Cornell Capa

EXECUTIVE DIRECTOR,
THE INTERNATIONAL CENTER
OF PHOTOGRAPHY

Clarkson N. Potter, Inc. / Publishers

DISTRIBUTED BY CROWN PUBLISHERS, INC.

NEW YORK

The quotation on page 25 is from *The Hidden Order of Art,* by Anton Ehrenzweig. Berkeley and Los Angeles: University of California Press, 1967.

The quotation on pages 29–30 is from *On Photography,* by Susan Sontag. New York: Farrar, Straus & Giroux, 1977.

The quotation on page 31 is from *Era of Exploration,* by Weston J. Naef. Buffalo: Albright-Knox Art Gallery; New York: Metropolitan Museum of Art, 1975.

Inquiries should be addressed to Clarkson N. Potter, Inc., One Park Avenue, New York, New York 10016.

Printed in the United States of America

Published simultaneously in Canada by General Publishing Company Limited

Library of Congress Cataloging in Publication Data

Whelan, Richard.
  Double take.

  Includes index.
  1. Photography, Artistic—History and criticism.
I. Title.
TR642.W46 1981   770   81-11903

ISBN: 0-517-543826 (cloth)
      0-517-545691 (paper)

Designed by Hermann Strohbach

10 9 8 7 6 5 4 3 2 1

First Edition

To R.L.S.

CONTENTS

FOREWORD

When Richard Whelan first approached us with his fresh and intriguing idea to unravel the inherent mystery of photography, I realized that it would be the basis for a most instructive opportunity—not only for the publication of a book, but for an exhibition at the International Center of Photography. The questions he raises have always plagued photographers and those interested in the medium. What and who create the photograph—the photographer, the camera, the subject? Is it possible that the photographer's approach is not unique, that the image is not unique?

Double Take, photographs of the same subject by different photographers, poses interesting questions. What makes the difference between two views of the same subject? Is it style, the light, the passage of time, the choice of film, the concept?

Richard Whelan has searched for answers to these seemingly simple questions. In the process, he has found and seen the connections inherent in seventy pairs of photographs by sixty-two well-known photographers, producing an incisive handbook on photography. In nontechnical terms, this book teaches us more about photography, more about seeing, than a score of other books. The history of photography will be well served by the many questions raised and answered through this investigative work.

It is a witty detective story in which the *corpus delicti* is pleasant to view. It is a visual adventure that amuses and instructs. In an odd sort of way, it is like photography, a magical process that is crammed through and through with unexpected pleasures and surprises.

Cornell Capa
Executive Director
International Center of Photography

PREFACE

The idea for this book was triggered by the monographs on photographers that began to appear in great numbers in the early 1970s, for it was in those volumes that I first discovered photographic doubles. My initial encounter occurred when I realized that the Christopher Street shopfront depicted in a photograph in André Kertész's 1972 book *Sixty Years of Photography* was the same as that in a photograph included in Berenice Abbott's 1970 retrospective monograph. The 1973 reprinting of Abbott's classic book *Changing New York*, originally published in 1939, brought to my attention her photograph of the doorway at 204 West Thirteenth Street, which matched up with a Walker Evans photograph in the catalog of his 1971 Museum of Modern Art retrospective. After a few more chance discoveries, I decided to become an active pursuer of photographic pairs. Finally, during 1979 and 1980, I completed a systematic search through all the monographs, surveys, and exhibition catalogs that I felt were important, as well as through many periodicals and auction catalogs. This procedure yielded several hundred pairs, from which the seventy reproduced here were chosen, using the following criteria:

- Both photographers represented in each pair had to be widely recognized as important camera artists.

- Both photographs in each pair had to be strong—even if in some cases they are not quite equally strong. I wanted to avoid comparisons where quality was the crucial differentiating factor.

- The photographs in each pair had to be as similar as possible, and yet significantly different. At the same time, I wanted to include as wide a variety of conceptions of similarity as possible without lapsing into visual puns. I have, therefore, included pairs in which both photographs depict precisely the same subject, others that deal with the same generic subject or photographic effect, and still others that record similar gestures and situations.

- As a general rule, no two photographers were to be paired up together more than once. The exceptions are Berenice Abbott and Walker Evans, Dorothea Lange and Ben Shahn, and Eadweard Muybridge and Carleton Watkins. These exceptions were made to demonstrate that the differences between these photographers remained fairly consistent.

Many great photographers are not included in the book simply because I did not find any photographs by them that matched up in a sufficiently interesting way with images by others.

The commentaries that accompany the pairs of

photographs provide some factual information and some subjective insights that I hope will provoke rather than assuage the reader's curiosity. In general, I have tried to avoid spelling out the obvious visual characteristics that distinguish the photographs in each pair, since I would like the reader to take an active role in comparing the photographs for himself or herself. For additional information about how an individual image fits into its maker's oeuvre, and for descriptions of the various kinds of prints represented here, the reader should consult the brief biographies and the notes on photographic processes at the back of the book. Specific

reference to the notes is made in the commentaries only when the processes are decisive in differentiating the photographs.

In the commentaries I have also tried to establish whether the photographer who made the later image might have known the earlier image, but it is usually impossible to pin down such information with any certainty. Most of the connections are necessarily speculative; I have most often been able to state only when and where it would have been *possible* for the second photographer to have seen the first photograph, though in some cases even that information remained elusive.

For the factual information presented throughout this book, I was greatly dependent on the standard photographic monographs, histories, catalogs, dictionaries, and technical books. My publisher decided, however, that the great number of footnotes that would have been necessary to document all of my sources would be inappropriate in this nonscholarly book. I regret, therefore, that I cannot offer more than general thanks and a blanket acknowledgment of my indebtedness to all those who may recognize here a borrowing from or a distillation of their researches and writings.

From among the many people who helped to make this book possible, I must single out a few for special thanks. Melanie Jackson of Candida Donadio and Associates gave me the encouragement that I needed to get started on the book, found a publisher, and followed through with advice, criticism, and moral support as the work progressed. Ron Schick, picture editor of *Portfolio* magazine, and Julia Van Haaften, curator of the New York Public Library's photographic collection, both responded with extraordinary patience and generosity to my many queries about picture sources and technical matters. They both also provided many helpful observations about the introductory essay and the selection of images. At a time when the gathering of copy prints for the book was beginning to look like an impossible task, Marie Withers, registrar of the Lunn Gallery in Washington, D.C., graciously provided enough advice and prints to enable me to regain my optimism and momentum.

Toby Quitslund proffered hospitality and guidance in Washington. Susan Kismaric, Associate Curator in the Department of Photography at the Museum of Modern Art, and Anne Horton, head of the Photography Department at Sotheby Parke Bernet, Inc., were both extremely generous with their expertise and with the resources of their departments. And for adding a whole new dimension—that of an exhibition—to my project, I am most grateful to Cornell Capa, Executive Director of the International Center of Photography, and to William A. Ewing, the Director of Exhibitions at the ICP.

For their valuable insights concerning the introductory essay and the pairs of photographs, I must particularly thank Isolde McNicholl, Dona Nelson, and Richard Shirk. Others whose reactions to the photographs were especially helpful and encouraging include Seymour Bernstein, Steve Ellis, Maria Morris Hambourg, Lynde Lafler, Donald Lorimer, Amanda Means, and Donald Van Hook.

I wish to extend sincere thanks to all of the following people, who helped me to locate original prints, who provided copy prints, who granted permission to reproduce the images or arranged for such permission, and/or who assisted me in tracking down information: Carla Ash, Joseph E. Seagram & Sons, Inc., New York; Miles Barth, International Center of Photography, New York; Janet Borden, Robert Freidus Gallery, New York; David Boyce, Sidney Janis Gallery, New York; Tom Brazil, Magnum Photos, Inc., New York; Esther Bromberg, Museum of the City of New York; Amy Brown, Julian Bach Literary Agency; Peter C. Bunnell, Princeton University, Princeton, New Jersey; Robert Cusie, Prakapas Gallery, New York; Marya Dalrymple, Harry N. Abrams, Inc., New York; King Dexter, Assistant to Ansel Adams, Carmel, California; Penelope Dixon, Phillips Auctioneers, New York; John Paul Driscoll, William Lane Foundation, Leominster, Massachusetts; Evan Evans, Fetcham, Surrey, England; Mary E. Fanette, Department of Photography, The Museum of Modern Art, New York; Rosamund Felsen, Rosamund Felsen Gallery, Los Angeles; Barbara Galasso, Print Service, The International Museum of Photography at George Eastman House, Rochester, New York; Marnie Gillett, Light Gallery, New York; Suzanne Goldstein, Photo Researchers, New York; Karen Greenberg, Sander Gallery, Washington, D.C.; Thomas D. Grischkowsky, Rights and Reproductions, The Museum of Modern Art, New York; Maria Morris Hambourg, Department of Photography, The Museum of Modern Art, New York; Susan Harder, assistant to André Kertész, New York; Marvin Heiferman, Castelli Photographs, New York; John T. Hill, Executor of the Estate of Walker Evans, Bethany, Connecticut; Scott Hyde, New York, who made many of the copy prints; Betsy Jablow, Department of Photography, The Museum of Modern Art, New York; Paul Katz, New York; Jain Kelly, New York; William Larson, Tucson, Arizona; Linda Lennon, Witkin Gallery, New York; Joan Liftin, Magnum Photos, Inc., New York; Charles Lokey, The Oakland Museum, Oakland, California; Dennis Longwell, Marlborough Gallery, New York; Harry Lunn, Lunn Gallery, Washington, D.C.; Juliet Man Ray, Paris; Gina Medcalf, Sotheby Parke Bernet, Inc., New York; Hattula Moholy-Nagy, Ann Arbor, Michigan; Weston Naef, Department of Prints and Photographs, The Metropolitan Museum of Art, New York; Richard Pare, Joseph E. Seagram & Sons, Inc., New York; Elizabeth Partridge and Rondal Partridge, The Imogen Cunningham Trust, Berkeley, California; Eugene Prakapas, Prakapas Gallery, New York; Davis Pratt, Fogg Art Museum, Harvard University, Cambridge, Massachusetts; Gertrude M. Prescott, Humanities Research Center, University of Texas, Austin; Crary Pullen, Phillips Auctioneers, New York; Gerd Sander, Sander Gallery, Washington, D.C.; Bernarda Shahn, Roosevelt, New Jersey; Marthe Smith, Life Picture Service, New York; Marjory Spoerri, Paul Strand Foundation, for permission to reproduce "Church, Ranchos de Taos, New Mexico, 1931," © 1971, 1976 The Paul Strand Foundation, as published in Paul Strand: *Sixty Years of Photographs,* Aperture, 1976, and "Side Porch, Vermont, 1947," © 1950, 1971, 1977 The Paul Strand Foundation, as published in Paul Strand: *Time in New England,* Aperture, 1980; Lucien Treillard, Paris; Louis L. Tucker and Ross Urquhart, Massachusetts Historical Society, Boston; Cole Weston, Carmel, California; Wilma Wilcox, Tirike, Kenya; Marjolaine Williams, Christie's East, New York; Lee Witkin and Ed Yankov, Witkin Gallery, New York; and Virginia Zabriskie, Zabriskie Gallery, New York.

I would like to thank the entire staff of the International Center of Photography, New York, for their assistance on the exhibition for which this book serves as the catalog. In addition to those people already mentioned specifically, I must offer special thanks to Barbara Burack, Development Coordinator; Ann Doherty, Director of Development; Steve Rooney, Assistant Director of Exhibitions; Ruth Silverman, Assistant Curator; Anna Winand, Executive Assistant; and Jacqui Wong, Curatorial Assistant. Special thanks are due to Sharon Gallagher, who did most of the work of obtaining vintage prints for the exhibition.

At Clarkson N. Potter, Inc., I am especially grateful to Michael Fragnito for championing the manuscript when it was first submitted and then following through with great care; to Anne Zeman for her continuing support; to Hermann Strohbach for admirably solving the challenging design problems posed by the juxtaposition of photographs and text; to George Oehl for attending to many details in the preparation of the manuscript; to Anne Ficklen for supervising the copyediting and proofreading; to Teresa Nicholas for her expert guidance in production; and, above all, to my editor, Nancy Novogrod, who firmly but tactfully steered my text back onto the right track whenever I started to lead it astray. Whatever infelicities of phrase or eccentricities of thought remain in the book must be blamed on my own stubbornness.

NOTES ON CAPTIONS

The sizes given here are those of typical vintage prints, though an image may exist in prints of varying sizes, depending on enlargement. All measurements are in inches, with height preceding width.

When two credits are given for a single photograph, the first supplied the copy print for reproduction and the second granted permission to reproduce the image. The sources of the copy prints, as noted in the captions, may in some cases differ from the sources of the vintage prints displayed at the *Double Take* exhibit at the International Center of Photography. The following abbreviations have been used for sources:

AIC: The Art Institute of Chicago
CCA: The Canadian Center for Architecture, Montreal
Christie's: Christie's East, New York
Cunningham Trust: The Imogen Cunningham Trust, Berkeley, California
Felsen Gallery: Rosamund Felsen Gallery, Los Angeles, California
Fogg: Fogg Art Museum, Harvard University, Cambridge, Massachusetts
FP: Fondazione Primoli, Rome
Freidus Gallery: Robert Freidus Gallery, New York
HRC/UT: Humanities Research Center, University of Texas, Austin
ICP: International Center of Photography, New York
IMP/GEH: International Museum of Photography at George Eastman House, Rochester, New York
Janis Gallery: Sidney Janis Gallery, New York

Lane Foundation: William H. Lane Foundation, Leominster, Massachusetts
LC: Department of Prints and Photographs, Library of Congress, Washington, D.C.
Life: Life Picture Service, Time Inc., New York
Lunn Gallery: Lunn Gallery, Washington, D.C.
Magnum: Magnum Photos, Inc., New York
MC: Musée Carnavalet, Paris
MCNY: Museum of the City of New York
MHS: Massachusetts Historical Society, Boston
MMA: Metropolitan Museum of Art, New York
MMA, Stieglitz: Metropolitan Museum of Art, New York. Alfred Stieglitz Collection
MoMA: Collection, The Museum of Modern Art, New York
MoMA, Abbott-Levy: Collection, The Museum of Modern Art, New York. Abbott-Levy Collection. Partial gift of Shirley C. Burden
MoMA/CAW: Restrike made by the Chicago Albumen Works in 1978 from the original negative in the collection of The Museum of Modern Art, New York
MWA: Reproduction courtesy The Minor White Archive, Princeton University, Princeton, New Jersey
NMS: Nationalmuseum, Stockholm, Sweden
NYPL: Rare Books Division, The New York Public Library
OM: Oakland Museum, Oakland, California
Phillips: Phillips Auctioneers, New York
Prakapas Gallery: Prakapas Gallery, New York
Sander Gallery: Sander Gallery, Washington, D.C.
SFP: Société Française de Photographie, Paris
Sotheby's: Sotheby Parke Bernet, New York
UCB: Bancroft Library, University of California, Berkeley
Witkin Gallery: Witkin Gallery, New York
Zabriskie Gallery: Zabriskie Gallery, New York and Paris

INTRODUCTION

I am always myself and must naturally be present in my work. The beards and eyebrows of the old masters cannot grow on my face. The lungs and bowels of the old masters cannot be transferred into my body. I express my own lungs and bowels and show my own beard and eyebrows. If it happens that my work approaches that of some old painter, it is he who comes close to me, not I who am imitating him. I have got it by nature, and there is no one among the old masters whom I cannot follow and transform.

Tao-chi (Chinese, seventeenth century)

The pairs of photographs in this book may, at first glance, induce a mild sense of disorientation. Are we or are we not seeing two related records of the same place, the same object, or the same event? Was there a lapse of seconds or of years between the instants in which the two photographs were made? In order to get our bearings, we must pin down the similarities and differences between the photographs, isolating and defining the quirks of each—a process that forces us to look more carefully than we might otherwise.

Discovering that a well-known photograph has an analogue is a bit like discovering that someone we know has a double—a stranger who bears him a striking and baffling resemblance. Even if the doubles turn out to be related to one another—and many of the paired photographs in this book do turn out to be historical cousins—the memory of the discovery can remain disturbing. It is no wonder that doubles and twins are universally surrounded with superstitions, for they challenge our fundamental, steadying sense of individuality. One bristles at any implication that anyone—especially oneself—may not be unique. We even bring a similar attitude to works of art, those supreme tokens of individuality, in which we equate value with uniqueness.

If we happen to see a pair of twins or doubles together, we automatically scan their faces for some reassuring difference that will break the spell of duplication. Through the process of back-and-forth comparison we are certain to perceive qualities and details that we might have missed if we had seen either person alone. In such a situation, subtleties become decisive—and hence apparent. The same thing should happen in looking at the pairs of photographs in this book.

Anyone who knows Ansel Adams's great photograph of the ruined pueblos in the Canyon de Chelly in Arizona *(see page 63)* is likely to experience a dislocating sense of *déjà vu* when he first stumbles on Timothy O'Sullivan's photograph of the same ruins *(see page 62)*. The discoverer of the doubles may wonder whether Adams could have known O'Sullivan's photograph—and, if so, whether he was paying homage to O'Sullivan or competing with him. Or was it just an extraordinary coincidence that two great photographers happened to photograph the same ruins? After the initial surprise has worn off, the viewer will surely get down to specific differences and perceive how dissimilar the two photographs really are, despite the identity of the subject. His perception of both images will have been permanently changed, for he will have glimpsed the range of possibilities that confronted both photographers. Each photograph will seem more integrally tied to the creative process than it did before the discovery of its double.

All perception is by nature comparative; we constantly check the unknown against the known, the new against the old, the large against the small, the specific against the general, one twin against the other. Comparison is such an important function that the ability to perceive similarities and differences is often used by psychologists as a measure of intelligence. The more creative the mind, the greater the agility in seeing correspondence between disparate people, objects, and situations. Such perceptions are the soul of wit and metaphor. Our discoveries of connections are surely among our greatest intellectual and artistic pleasures, for similes, affinities, sequences, and even puns all give us a sense of underlying order and fraternity. Conversely, the finer the tuning of the mind, the more resistance there is to allowing similar things to pass as exact doubles. Our instinctive fear of imitators and impostors is the basis of connoisseurship.

In each of the juxtapositions here, it may appear as if the cameras of two photographers have almost converged momentarily. These instances of identity, or at least of strong affinity, of subject matter raise questions of influence and coincidence and point to crosscurrents in the history of photography. Art history, which includes the history of photography, is essentially the study of the origin, transmission, transformation, and transcendence of styles and motifs. Insofar as it is concerned with questions of uniqueness versus influence, the nature of the discipline is comparative. It follows, therefore, that the basic unit of discussion in art history is the pair of works. To practice his expertise, the art historian must mentally or physically place the work under consideration beside others. Only on the basis of comparisons of details and overall impact can he decide whether an unsigned work conforms to the style of signed works by the artist to whom it is attributed or whether an undated work was a prototype or a derivative.

The purpose of this book is not merely to point out that great photographers have frequently learned from one another. Although many of the pairs document instances of influence—providing evidence of connections between such masters as Alfred Stieglitz and Edward Steichen, Charles Sheeler and Walker Evans, Edward Weston and Ansel Adams—many others arise from coincidence. (There is, for instance, no explanation beyond coincidence of why, in 1929, André Kertész in France and Manuel Alvarez Bravo in Mexico, neither of whom knew the other's work, both photographed wooden circus horses in carts [*see pages 116 and 117.*]) The comparisons are intended not only to reveal similarities, but also, more important, to make it easier for the reader to perceive the nuances that *distinguish* similar treatments of similar

subjects. It is in these subtleties that we find the essence of each photograph's originality. The question of influence is interesting only insofar as it allows us to glimpse the mechanics of creativity, to watch an idea being transformed and revitalized.

The differences between these photographs of identical or similar subjects raise one of the central issues of this book: that of the nature of style in photography. Many critics believe that photographic style is strictly a matter of consistently choosing certain kinds of subjects. They assume that the camera simply records these subjects, which impose particular styles that are somehow intrinsic to the subjects themselves. The pairs in this book should help to dispel that misconception, for the reader who looks carefully will have no difficulty in recognizing that the photographs in each pair, even if they focus on precisely the same subject, differ in stance, details, technique, lighting, mood, and so on. In short, they differ in style. These intensely subjective factors contribute as much to the overall impact of a photograph as does the choice of what to photograph. A photographer's style and his choice of subject matter are inextricably related, but they do not amount to the same thing.

The question of the relationship between style and subject matter in photography, as in any other medium of expression, is a variation on the perennial chicken-and-egg conundrum of form and content. Style, which determines the form of content, and subject matter, which determines the content of form, constitute an organic unity within every photograph. That unity arises from the fact that a photographer's background, character, intelligence, and sensibility will determine how he perceives the world, and his perceptions will determine both *what* he will choose to photograph and *how* he will photograph it.

Every photographer will respond to some subjects more than to others, and he will respond only to some aspects of each of those subjects. If we are to interpret photographs not only as works of art but also as sources of information about external reality, we must recognize the ways in which a photographer's sensibility is specialized. We need to develop a sense of the photographer's style both to gain insights into his creative personality and to evaluate his biases—for a photograph tells us as much about the photographer as it does about the subject.

The juxtapositions in this book may initially seem to emphasize the points of similarity between the photographs and to force the rest of their content into the background, but the residue that remains after the similarities have flashed out may be as close to a pure extract of the photographers' styles as we can obtain.

Every pair of photographs of identical subjects implies a triangle connecting the two photographs and their subject. Although many of the most important questions raised by the pairs concern the relationships between the two photographs, we must not lose sight of the line that connects each photograph to its subject. Before we consider in depth the implications of the comparisons, we should try to answer the basic questions of what photographs are and how, in general, they relate to their subjects.

WHAT IS A PHOTOGRAPH?

Reduced to their lowest common denominator, photographs are usually the concrete results of a photographer's response to a stimulus—a photographer being defined as anyone who is prepared at a given moment to respond to a stimulus by using a camera. The immediate stimulus is usually the visual perception of something (the subject), but the full range of emotions, associations, and memories (including memories of other photographs) that the subject evokes are part of the stimulus complex and will all affect how the photographer actually perceives the subject—and hence whether and how he will choose to photograph it.

Perhaps the most puzzling element of the stimulus complex is the desire to make a photograph in the first place. In recent years, theoreticians of photography have advanced a great many speculations about why people feel the need to make photographs: to endow the moment recorded with a sort of deep-frozen immortality, to fragment experience into manageable pieces, to insulate oneself from new experiences (like travelers who never *really* look at anything—they just take photographs), to analyze episodes of life, to exercise a form of voyeuristic aggression, to transform experience into objects (photographs) that can be possessed and hoarded like money, to learn about the structure and meaning of the world, or simply to make aesthetically and intellectually provocative images.

The actual appearance of a photograph, whatever the photographer's reason for making it, will be profoundly affected by his reflexes, technical facility, and aesthetic sensibility—all of which will contribute to determining how he will compose the image, what kind of camera and film he will use, when he will trip the shutter, and how he will develop and print the negative. It is largely the cumulative effects of these decisions that differentiate the photographs in each pair in this book.

In a strictly technical sense, a modern black-and-white photograph is usually a piece of paper that has been coated with gelatin or resin holding grains of light-sensitive silver halides (mostly silver bromide and silver chloride) in emulsion. The process of photography is essentially a matter of controlling the darkening of those silver halides, first on the negative and then on the print, so that the finished print records the light and dark values of the subject in accordance with the photographer's intentions. The result is a literal but miniature transcription—or, more accurately, a transposition from the major key of full-color, binocular, three-dimensional human vision to the minor key of black-and-white, monocular, two-dimensional camera vision—of every detail of the scene that was framed in the viewfinder and in focus when the photographer pressed the shutter release.

Every photograph is a picture of something; it records some aspect of the appearance of external reality. An image cannot even be formed on film unless there are objects in the camera's field of vision to reflect light and to cast shadows. Double exposure prints, photomontages, and composite prints made from parts of several different negatives, however bizarre they may seem, all begin with straightforward images and can usually be analyzed into their components. Even the most abstract-seeming photographs are usually made by photographing objects so that they become difficult to recognize. The photographer, however concerned with pure form he may be, must decide *what* to photograph, and he must consider the literal implications of his subject.

As the very term "photo*graphy*" implies, photographs represent an extension of the long tradition of the graphic arts. Like woodcuts, copper-plate engravings, etchings, aquatints, mezzotints, lithographs, and other "exactly repeatable pictorial statements," most photographs are pieces of paper bearing mechanically and chemically transferred images. Both photography and the traditional graphic arts produce numerous prints (even the terms are the same) from a matrix—a woodblock, metal plate, or lithographic stone in the graphic media and a negative in photography. Two of the traditional graphic processes—etching and aquatint—even involve "developing" the metal plate in an acid bath to bring out the image so that it can be printed, and a lithographic drawing must be "fixed" chemically so that it will not wipe off the stone. All the traditional graphic processes involve printing on a mechanical press. Photography was thus by no means the first chemical and mechanical art form.

On account of their long-standing, intimate association with the printed word, both photography and the traditional graphic arts have been, throughout most of their histories, primarily black-and-white media. Because, well into the twentieth century, color photographs could not be reproduced both accurately and cheaply on the printed page, and because publishing has been the primary means of disseminating photographic images, there was, until the 1940s, great pressure for photography to remain monochromatic. Even today, the economics of publishing favor black-and-white photographs. The majority of photographic images that any of us has seen have probably not been original prints on photographic paper—or even color illustrations—but rather halftone reproductions printed, like type and line engravings, with black printer's ink on ordinary paper.

A woodcut or an etching usually took much less time to make than did a highly finished painting, and low-cost prints reached a wide popular audience. For centuries, therefore, artists were much freer to indulge their fancy in choosing subjects when they worked in the graphic media than when they painted. In fact, although the great majority of European paintings were portraits, nudes, and historical scenes made for the aristocracy and religious scenes made for the church, just about *everything*—from a casually observed scene to a single household object—was a possible subject for a print. Graphic artists made topographical and scientific studies, fashion plates, pictures of exotic people and places, images of current events, and advertise-ments, as well as works that fall into the traditional artistic categories of portraits, nudes, landscapes, still lifes, genre scenes, religious and historical images, and allegories.

Photography has inherited almost the entire range of subject matter that formerly belonged to the graphic arts. Indeed, photography gradually displaced the traditional graphic media from virtually all of their nonartistic roles, and even from many of their artistic ones. Since the late 1890s, when halftone reproductions of photographs in books and magazines became commonplace, the old graphic media have been used almost exclusively to make images that are solely intended to be works of art.

Throughout its history, photography has been plagued by the question, "Can a picture made by a machine (i.e., a camera) be a work of art?" Photographs are not, however, made by cameras; they are made by people who use cameras to serve their expressive needs. Works of art are possible in any medium (be it painting, photography, video, or whatever), but they are guaranteed in none. Furthermore the sophistication of the photographer's equipment has nothing to do with whether or not he will make photographs that hold up as works of art. The photographer's intelligence, sensitivity, character, imagination, and spirit are far more important than fancy equipment.

Even when photographs succeed as works of art, they are hardly ever *just* works of art. Virtually every photograph that functions as a work of art will also function as a document about a specific place, time, object, event, person, or group of persons. It may also function as a mnemonic aid for anyone who has had direct contact with the subject, as a substitute of greater or lesser effectiveness for such contact, as the basis for all sorts of fantasies, as an illustration in many different contexts (each of which will change the meaning of the photograph), or as an almost magical talisman from the past. Any or all of these functions may affect the way we see any given photograph. Perhaps no other artistic or communicative medium is quite so ambiguous and elusive.

OBJECTIVITY AND SUBJECTIVITY: THE SPLIT PERSONALITY OF PHOTOGRAPHY

Photography is a medium with a profoundly split personality, torn between intense objectivity and intense subjectivity. *All* photographs are both ob-jective reports and subjective expressions—facts and fictions. Insofar as photographs supply the viewer with highly detailed, precise, mechanically

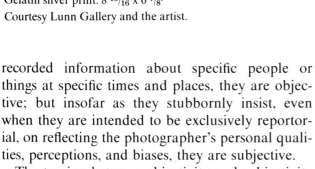

Berenice Abbott,
Repair Shop, 19 Christopher Street, New York, late 1940s.
Gelatin silver print. 8 ¹³/₁₆ x 6 ⁷/₈.
Courtesy Lunn Gallery and the artist.

André Kertész,
Christopher Street, New York, 1950.
Gelatin silver print. 8½ x 5⅜.
© André Kertész.

recorded information about specific people or things at specific times and places, they are objective; but insofar as they stubbornly insist, even when they are intended to be exclusively reportorial, on reflecting the photographer's personal qualities, perceptions, and biases, they are subjective.

The tension between objectivity and subjectivity will become apparent if we compare the photographs that Berenice Abbott and André Kertész made of the same shopfront in the Greenwich Village section of New York City. Abbott's photograph appears at first to be a straightforward, objective statement, but far from presenting an image of the shopfront as it would have appeared to anyone passing by at the time, her photograph lifts it out of context and transforms it. Indeed, the solidity of the composition (made all the more solid by its having been carefully composed on the ground glass of an old-fashioned, tripod-mounted

view camera) and the exclusion of any people whose clothes might date the image might lead one to think, if the photograph were reproduced without a caption, that it had been made in the nineteenth century rather than in the late 1940s. Nineteenth-century photographs of cities often made the streets and sidewalks look deserted, since the processes of the time necessitated such long exposures that the forms of moving pedestrians, horses, or vehicles could not be recorded. Abbott's film, however, would have been fast enough to freeze pedestrians if she had chosen to include any.

Abbott, whose temperament is essentially like that of a nineteenth-century American pioneer or a scientist, reacted strongly against the aesthetics of Surrealism and Constructivism, to which she had been exposed in Paris during the 1920s. Hence, ironically, the very stance of objectivity that shapes her photograph of the shopfront clearly reflects her

19

own intransigently down-to-earth, head-on, no-nonsense personality.

While Abbott strove to photograph the shopfront *as it was*, she nevertheless made the decision to photograph that particular facade at that particular moment in that particular way. At another time, the light might have been different, the hands of the clock and the delivery cart might have been in different positions, and Abbott might have been in a different mood that would have altered her decisions. Furthermore, although Abbott made her photograph to be reproduced in a book entitled *Greenwich Village Today and Yesterday*, written by Henry Wysham Lanier and published in 1949, her photograph doesn't feel like a mere illustration of a representative aspect of the old neighborhood. It is hard to resist reading the photograph as an allegory on old-fashioned precision in the midst of modern carelessness—precision being symbolized by the huge clock with its bold, crisp numerals and hands, by the polishing machine behind the right corner of the window, and by the balances covered with bell jars at the left; and carelessness being symbolized by the cracked, bespattered, and littered sidewalk. It is tempting to imagine that Abbott identified her own sensibility with that of the unseen proprietor of that tidy shop.

Like Abbott, Hungarian-born André Kertész photographed in Paris during the 1920s before moving to New York. But unlike Abbott, Kertész's abiding concerns have been gesture, sentiment, striking or witty juxtapositions, and unsettling predicaments. In general, his intentions have been as subjective as Abbott's have been objective, and his sensibility is as modernistic as Abbott's is traditional.

Kertész's photograph of the shopfront is clearly a twentieth-century image. For one thing, it has the immediacy of a shot made with a fast, versatile, hand-held 35mm camera—the camera that, following its appearance on the market in 1925, Kertész was one of the first to raise from the status of an amateur's toy to that of the standard instrument of photojournalists and serious photographers. Despite the presence of the clock, Abbott's unpopulated photograph conveys a certain sense of timelessness, but the shadow of the passerby whose foot is just barely inside the frame of Kertész's photograph emphasizes that his image has captured a fleeting moment—three minutes and some odd seconds past two o'clock on a sunny afternoon.

Kertész has made a clearly focused and informative image of the shopfront and the delivery cart, and yet he was surely much less interested in showing us what the facade and cart looked like in themselves than he was in framing the somewhat surreal juxtaposition of the clock and the twelve-spoked wheel. The similarity of these forms—in shape, size, and organization—creates a tremendous tension that is heightened by the shadow that has ominously entered this twilight zone.

Although Kertész had probably seen Abbott's photograph in her 1949 book, both photographers *found* their subjects and *created* their images. Abbott's picture, however, deceptively gives the impression of having been more found than created, since her emphasis was on conveying information about her subject. In contrast, Kertész's seems more created than found, since his emphasis was on making an extraordinary photograph that would be entirely self-referential. Abbott's photograph purports to show us the essential appearance of a place that she carefully identifies in her caption as a repair shop located at 19 Christopher Street in New York City, but it wouldn't significantly change our perception of the Kertész if his caption happened to say "Paris" rather than "New York." Finally, the very fact that Kertész could make such a radically different photograph of the same facade and cart proves how intensely subjective Abbott's ostensibly objective photograph really is.

Every photograph is simultaneously a mirror that reflects the subjectivity of the photographer's interior life and a window that looks objectively out onto some aspect of the external world. We might, therefore, take a pair of reflected self-portraits by Imogen Cunningham and Lee Friedlander as paradigms of the art of photography. In each picture, we see the photographer's reflection caught in a play of windows and mirrors that creates an image of great ambiguity, complexity, and wit.

Both photographers recorded situations that they half found and half created, since the windows and mirrors were there all along, but the photographers obviously weren't reflected in them until they put themselves in position to make their photographs. Moreover, it took the photographers' rich imaginations to realize that they could use these jumbled configurations of windows and mirrors, which were not intrinsically of any particular interest, as the raw material for fascinating photographs. Both Cunningham and Friedlander used these windows and mirrors to make photographs that are at the same time highly objective and highly subjective

Imogen Cunningham,
Self-Portrait on Geary Street, San Francisco, 1958.
Gelatin silver print. 9½ x 7½ inches.
Courtesy Cunningham Trust.

Lee Friedlander,
New Orleans, 1968.
Gelatin silver print. 7 x 10¾.
Courtesy Freidus Gallery and the artist.

records of a situation. The photographs are straightforward, sharply focused, and unmanipulated (i.e., they were not double exposed or transformed with darkroom tricks). And yet each is filled with mystery and with the photographer's presence as both creator and subject. They both dramatically embody and symbolize the ambiguity of all photographs.

The ambiguity of objectivity and subjectivity is to be found in all works of art, but photographs reflect this split with special poignancy because they convey a uniquely illusory sense of the subject's objective presence, thereby intensifying the ambiguity. This ambiguity affects us profoundly because it echoes the ambiguity that pervades the human condition. We are all caught in the dilemma of objective knowledge versus subjective distortion; we all operate with an inseparable mix of consciousness and unconsciousness, intellect and emotion, generalities and specifics, idealism and realism. Ambiguity is even built into the very structure of our bicameral brains, in which the right hemisphere governs processes that are predomi-

nantly subjective, intuitive, and holistic, while the left governs those that are more objective, logical, and analytical. In actuality, every action is shaped by the interaction of the two hemispheres as well as by that of the various levels of consciousness.

Virtually all theories of aesthetics posit that works of art balance a multitude of dualities—such as subjectivity and objectivity, conception and execution, content and form, imagination and truth, abstraction and representation—in a state of fluid, ambiguous unity. This ambiguity not only mirrors the human existential balancing act but also keeps works of art open-ended, resisting explanation and analysis. Indeed, the more we try to analyze a work of art, the more ambiguous and elusive it becomes. Such elusiveness is so essential to works of art that it is one of the primary criteria in determining whether or not an image succeeds as art. It is this combination of clarity and ambiguity, of the familiar and the unfamiliar, of the ordinary and extraordinary that disorients us, throws us off balance, breaks down our rational defenses, and triggers epiphanies when we look at works of art.

BLACK-AND-WHITE PHOTOGRAPHY AND THE FORM OF AN INSTANT

Black-and-white photographs are filled with tensions between objectivity and subjectivity, but they also disorient us by depriving us of many of the clues on which we usually depend for our interpretations of visual stimuli. They remove color; they substitute monocular vision (which flattens out space) for binocular vision (which is necessary for the accurate perception of distance and depth); they present a fixed focus and perspective rather than the constantly shifting and compensating effects of normal, conscious scanning vision; and they eliminate peripheral vision. They radically fragment experience and remove individual segments from their space/time contexts, making a rigidly circumscribed view, taken in a split second, stand for an entire life or place or event. To the extent that these distortions are present in all black-and-white photographs, the medium is undeniably *part* of the message. It's a wonder that we can read and interpret photographs at all and relate them to the world that we see with our naked eyes.

Paradoxically, the transposition of colors into black, white, and shades of gray contributes to a photograph's clarity as well as to its ambiguity, since black-and-white photographs not only eliminate the important clues that colors provide for identifying objects, but also cut through the distractions of color that keep our eyes on the surface of things. When we look at a *color* photograph, we see, first and foremost, *colors* and their interrelationships. When we look at black-and-white photographs, we see, first and foremost, *forms* and their interrelationships.

Black-and-white photographs are inherently both more ambiguous and more analytical than are color photographs. As analytical aids, black-and-white photographs are like X-ray plates that record a penetration through the surface of appearances to the bones of form and structure. The contemporary photographer Garry Winogrand has said that he makes photographs "to see what things will look like photographed." Although this statement may sound evasive or tautological, it actually makes every bit as much sense as if a doctor were to say that he was going to take an X-ray to see what some part of a patient's body would look like X-rayed.

Although most people assume that photographs record precisely what the photographer sees at the moment he presses the shutter button of his camera, the truth of the matter is that the photographer himself cannot fully know what his photograph will look like until he has developed the negative and made a satisfactory print of it. If the photographer is working quickly with a small camera, the photograph is sure to contain details of which he was not consciously aware, and even if he is working slowly with a large view camera, his total previsualization of the photograph will be blocked somewhat by the fact that the image will appear upside down on the ground-glass screen of his camera. The photographer can learn to judge and to compensate for the quirks of his camera and film, but he can never fully anticipate what his picture will look like if he is making stop-action photographs of things that are moving faster than the naked eye can register them or if he is making time-exposures of anything that might move, even so slowly that the movement would normally be imperceptible. Another element of risk is added by the fact that a photographer usually cannot see his subject at the moment of exposure. In the single lens reflex (the standard 35mm camera), the mirror that ordinarily covers the film and reflects the image into the viewfinder rises to expose the film and covers the viewfinder—thereby blocking the photographer's vision of his subject. Similarly, when a photographer uses a view camera, he must frame and focus the image before inserting the plate, which cuts off his view. This is not a serious problem in the case of the view camera, which is most often used to photograph static subjects, but photographers who shoot rapidly changing scenes with single lens reflex cameras must develop the ability to anticipate the gestures that they will capture on their film. As new photographers say, "If you saw it, you missed it."

The total effect of the variations between the way the naked eye sees a scene and the way the camera records it is so unpredictable that a considerable element of what appears to be chance enters into every act of photographing. Even the most experienced photographer has to be a shrewd and sportive gambler, willing to take his chances while trying to beat the system. He must be willing to be fascinated rather than disappointed by the discrepancies between the picture he gets and the picture he thought and hoped he was getting.

The somewhat unpredictable structure that is revealed by a photograph is that of the interaction among three factors: (1) the subject as it existed in itself at the moment in which the photograph was made, (2) the subject as it was perceived by the photographer at that moment, and (3) the subject as it was recorded by the camera. The cumulative effect of this interaction calls to mind the Uncertainty Principle that the nuclear physicist Werner Heisenberg published in 1927. This principle states that the means of observing and measuring the movements of atomic particles affect those movements in an unpredictable way that makes it impossible to obtain accurate, simultaneous measurements of both the position of a particle (such as an electron) and its velocity. The Uncertainty Principle is, in effect, a confirmation within the realm of the physical sciences of the effects of the interaction among the subject, the photographer, and his camera.

To characterize the ineluctable relationship among all events that take place within a given moment, the psychologist C. G. Jung used the term "synchronicity." In his introduction to one edition of the *I Ching* (the ancient Chinese classic that offers ambivalent advice by interpreting symbolic patterns of solid and broken lines—called hexagrams—that the consulter arrives at by chance), Jung says of synchronicity that it "takes the coincidence of events in space and time as meaning something more than chance, namely, a peculiar interdependence of objective events among themselves as well as with the subjective (psychic) states of the observer or observers." Jung goes on to say that "the hexagram was understood to be an indicator of the essential situation prevailing in the moment of its origin."

By extension, we might say that, as one of their many functions, photographs fulfill for us the role that hexagrams fulfilled for the ancient Chinese. In fact, in his description of the relationship between a hexagram and the moment when the consulter constructs it—by throwing sticks or coins to arrive at numbers that determine the configuration—Jung could just as easily be speaking of photographs. "The Chinese picture [i.e., conception] of the moment," he wrote, "encompasses everything down to the minutest nonsensical detail, because all of the ingredients make up the observed moment."

Within a painting, everything is related to everything else because of the painter's conscious decisions. Within a photograph, however, everything is related both by the photographer's decisions and by the recorded fact of simultaneity, or, as Jung would put it, "synchronicity." The photographer may compose his picture so that things that he sees as related to one another will be included together in the photograph, but there will usually also be numerous other details of which the photographer could not have been consciously aware at the moment when he released the shutter of his camera.

What relationship do these unexpected details bear to the selected ones? If we accept the claim that everything that occurs within an observed moment is somehow related, then the very act of recording these apparently random occurrences in a photograph endows them with meaning. The extraordinary echoes of shapes that one often finds within photographs of street scenes, for instance, are then not to be seen merely as arbitrary facts but as signs of the meaning that was set up by the photographer's interaction with the scene. By revealing order within even what appear to be randomly framed views, photographs can give us a unique glimpse of the inexorable logic of nature, of life, of the world.

PHOTOGRAPHY AND THE SUBCONSCIOUS

Conscious human vision is highly selective. When we look at a scene, we consciously see only what is most important to us and, to a great extent, only what we expect to see. But the camera, of course, records every detail of whatever is in front of the lens, without assessing the relative importance, interest, or meaning of the elements. In this respect, the camera comes very close to simulating human subconscious, or subliminal, vision—the functioning of which will greatly affect the photographer's handling of his subject. The photographer may not be *consciously* aware of all the details that will ap-

pear on the negative, but they nevertheless influence his decisions in the process of making the photograph, since they register in his subconscious mind through his subliminal vision.

The conscious mind, in effect, divides sensory information into discrete bits, sorts them, and evaluates them. The subconscious, on the other hand, scans and absorbs whole blocks of visual information more or less intact. Things that may appear ambiguous or incongruous to the censors of the conscious mind will be grasped without difficulty by the subconscious. While consciousness carefully establishes and maintains the differences between things, the subconscious breaks down differences and discovers the connections that surface in metaphor and wit. Moreover, as the British psychologist Anton Ehrenzweig has written, subconscious vision is "capable of scanning serial structures and gathering more information than a conscious scrutiny lasting a hundred times longer. With impartial acuity subliminal vision registers details irrespective of whether they belong to the figure or the ground." In the descriptions of all of these functions, one could substitute the word "camera" for every use of the words "subconscious" or "subliminal."

Insofar as the camera mechanically simulates subconscious vision, photographs bring an approximation of that vision, captured intact, before our eyes for conscious examination. Because black-and-white photographs eliminate distinctions of color, compress space, accentuate patterns of light and dark, catch the most fleeting nuances of gesture and expression, and register background details as clearly as those in the foreground, they offer a view of the world that is ordinarily inaccessible to consciousness. Their affinity to subconscious vision may even trigger a reflex response in the viewer's mind, opening up channels of access to related material buried in his own subconscious.

A photograph is like an externalized eidetic memory, which is an extremely vivid memory that a person endowed with eidetic recall (often called "photographic memory") forms after a very brief inspection of a picture. The resulting mental image is so detailed that, as the novelist and writer on psychology Arthur Koestler has described it, one can "count the buttons on a coat, the number of spokes on a wheel, and 'read' the letters in a foreign-language text forward or backward." Koestler goes on to point out that eidetic memory is commonly found only in children before the age of puberty: "The eidetic type of memory," he notes, "seems to be irretrievably lost, in all but exceptional cases, with the transition from the perceptual and affective to the conceptual and symbolic mentality." Pictorial memory, he states, belongs to an early stage of the development of both the individual and the human species. Photographs thus simulate a form of preconceptual memory to which most adults have lost access.

It is true, as Susan Sontag contends, that "photography is the only art that is natively surreal," but what renders a photograph surreal is not, as she argues, "its irrefutable pathos as a message from the past and the concreteness of its intimations

about social class," but rather its almost magical-seeming illusion of realism and its ability to achieve what we instinctively respond to as a synthesis of conscious and subconscious vision. Looking at any black-and-white photograph gives us a hint of what it might be like to look at a "still" from a dream. Indeed, although nobody is really certain whether we dream in black and white or in color, many psychologists agree that our dreams at the deepest levels of sleep seem to be colorless, while dreams that definitely involve some reference to color generally occur shortly before waking, when the dreamer is close to consciousness.

Color photographs, of course, record details as well as black-and-white ones do, but the monochromatic quality of the latter is apparently closer to unconscious perception. Although the psycho-physiological mechanisms of color perception are far from fully understood, it seems that the perception of relative brightness is more basic than the perception of color. Perhaps the reason that most serious photographers have until recently shunned color is that they have instinctively sensed not only that color photographs tend to be less powerfully ambiguous than black-and-white ones but also that they are closer to normal conscious vision.

The choice between black-and-white and color film is, then, not a matter of reactionism versus avant-gardism or of asceticism versus hedonism. Color and black-and-white photographs are actually *about* different things. Color photographs are disjunctive and sensual; black-and-whites are conjunctive and cerebral. The photographer who uses black-and-white film starts out with an advantage; his medium evidently offers easier access to the subconscious, with its overtones of surrealism and repressed emotions, the expression of which is an essential function of art. This access to the seething subconscious may help to explain why it is so difficult to imagine in anything but black and white the work of such photographers as Diane Arbus, in whose photographs there is an element of rapacious voyeurism, or Weegee, who was drawn to scenes of violence. Their photographs simply wouldn't have been as powerful or as disturbing in color. They would have been just grotesque or horrifying *pictures* rather than profoundly unsettling *photographs*.

The photographer who uses color film must work extraordinarily hard to make an image that resonates with anything like the kind of ambiguity and dreamlike, subconscious-simulating qualities that come naturally to black and white. It may be precisely an intuition of the magnitude of this challenge that began to attract so many sophisticated and adventurous photographers to color during the 1970s.

PHOTOGRAPHY AND THE CREATIVE PROCESS

In his analysis of the creative process, Anton Ehrenzweig distinguished three stages. In the first stage, the artist formulates his intentions, chooses his subject, and arrives at a conception of his work. In the second, he surrenders conscious control of the elements that he had projected into the work and discovers subconscious and seemingly accidental connections among both those elements and others outside the preconceived scope of the work. And in the final stage, the artist attempts to incorporate the often chaotic-seeming insights of the second stage into the conscious structure of the work—thus producing a work of art that integrates conscious and subconscious levels of experience.

Analyzing photography in terms of these three stages, we might say that after the photographer has selected his subject and conceptualized his photograph, the second stage begins when he is forced to deal on a reflex level with configurations, gestures, facial expressions, or light effects that are changing rapidly. The deepest level of relinquishing conscious control, however, comes when he presses the shutter button of his camera and transfers the actual formation of the image to the camera, which records with uncanny accuracy all the coincidences, "accidents," and formal interrelationships that the photographer may perceive only subliminally. The photographer can exercise his consciously selective vision only before and after the split second in which he actually makes the exposure, at which time he momentarily yields to all-inclusive camera vision. The camera may, in effect, mechanically circumvent some of the obstacles that might interfere with the artist's access to his creative subconscious if he were working in a different medium. Because of this automatic function of the camera, it is undeniably easier to make *good* black-and-white photographs than it is to make *good* paintings. Paradoxically, it does not follow that it is any easier to make *great* photographs than it is to make *great* paintings, for greatness is a matter of spirit rather than of technique.

A photographer will usually shoot a whole series of exposures of a subject, following action as it develops and experimenting with different angles, lighting, lenses, shutter speeds, and so on. Only after he has developed his negatives can he know for certain what he has got. He must then edit his contact sheets, a process that corresponds to Ehrenzweig's third stage, of which he says:

> It is this third phase of re-introjection when the independent existence of the work of art is felt most strongly. The work of art acts like another living person with whom we are conversing. . . . To accept the work's independent life requires a humility that is an essential part of creativity.

It is at this stage that the photographer must come to terms with the unexpected elements and effects in his images. He must remain open not only to the images that best fulfill his consciously preconceived intentions but also to those that are brought to life by things that may have registered and influenced his photographic decisions only subconsciously.

TECHNIQUE AND EXPRESSION IN PHOTOGRAPHY

A painter asserts his personality in every mark he makes on his canvas. At least some aspects of his brushwork, color, formal handling, and composition, insofar as they reflect his basic temperament and sensibility, tend to remain fairly constant throughout his career, giving a certain stylistic unity to all of his paintings, whatever their subjects. That formal, technical, and expressive constancy provides the basis of connoisseurship, which is postulated on the assumption that an artist, however dramatically his work may appear to change, remains essentially the same person throughout his life. Even in a career as filled with stylistic revolutions as was Picasso's, the art historian can easily find traits that relate the artist's latest paintings to his earliest. The constant qualities of an artist's work—both over the course of a lifetime and, more obviously, within the specific stylistic periods of his

Claude Monet,
La Grenouillère, 1869.
Oil on canvas. 29⅜ x 39¼.
MMA, H.O. Havemeyer Collection.

career—constitute a sort of artistic handwriting, which can be, in the case of an artist like Monet or Renoir, so instantly recognizable that it renders the painter's signature redundant.

The differences in the qualities of their colors provide important clues for distinguishing between paintings by Monet and Renoir, but even if we look at black-and-white reproductions of the canvases that the two men painted in 1869, when they set up their easels beside each other on the banks of La Grenouillère (literally, "the frog pond," a branch of the Seine at Croissy that was the site of a popular restaurant), anyone who has looked carefully at a few Monets and Renoirs should have no difficulty in determining, without looking at the signatures, which artist painted which canvas. All one really has to do is to look at the way the trees in the backgrounds are painted: Renoir's have the delicate, transparent brushiness that he brought from his years as a china painter and from his love of Boucher and Fragonard, while Monet's trees are opaque, flat, and stylized. Beyond that, Renoir, who loved to paint the hustle-bustle and fine clothes of bourgeois parties, has filled the center of his rather crowded composition with a voluptuous crowd of people, while Monet, who was much more interested in landscape than in people, painted his figures in a somewhat stiff and grudging style, reducing them to spindly counterweights in his relatively sparse, classically ordered composition. Furthermore, in the radically abstract, isolated brushstrokes with which Monet has painted the reflections on the water in this early work—in contrast to Renoir's more illusionistically liquid handling—we can see a premonition of the style of his late studies of water lilies.

The differences between the two paintings become all the more remarkable when we consider that the two painters had a standing agreement, whenever they worked together, to treat the scene before them as objectively as possible. But however earnestly they resolved to suppress their differences, the idiosyncrasies of their eyes and hands betrayed them. The human hand leaves its signature on everything it makes. Consistent—and therefore recognizable—traits are unavoidable. They creep even into the work of the cleverest forgers.

A painter shapes every mark on his canvas by a specific gesture. His gestures are cumulative; every brushstroke affects his decisions about the next. The making of one mark may even force the artist to go back and change areas already painted. A painting develops slowly across the surface of the canvas—like a glacier, utterly transforming the landscape, throwing up mountain ranges and dropping boulders in its path. The exposure of a photographic film, on the other hand, is like a flash of lightning; the energies build up and then are released in an instant.

The painter consciously makes the decisions that organize the elements of his composition in a particular configuration. If he finds one composition to be unsatisfactory, he can paint it out and try something else. But if a photographer deals largely with

Auguste Renoir,
La Grenouillère, 1869.
Oil on canvas. 26 x 31⅞.
NMS.

subjects that are constantly changing and beyond his control, and if he does not make the kind of direct, tactile, gestural marks that fill a painting with a sense of the artist's immediate presence, how can he make a picture that will express his artistic personality and intentions as well as a painting expresses those of its maker?

In this age of automatic cameras and commercial film processing, it is easy to lose sight of how many highly subjective decisions can go into the making of a photograph—each of those decisions leading to a *gesture* whose traces will reveal some aspect of the photographer's character. A photographer's style is the aggregate of these formal and technical—and yet ultimately expressive—gestures.

It can be extremely simple to make a photograph. As the advertisements for the automatic cameras that came to dominate the market during the 1970s tell us, you just have to select your subject, aim your camera, focus, and press the shutter button. Built-in computers will do the rest. Then you take your exposed film to the camera store or drugstore, wait a week or so, and pick up the finished prints or slides—though you won't even have to do that if you use a camera that produces finished prints. It is no wonder that most people in the world's industrially developed nations now regard the camera as little more than an appliance—the visual equivalent of the tape recorder.

It may, then, surprise many people to learn how many variables can go into the making of a photograph. Some of the most important are listed here,

not necessarily in the order in which the photographer must deal with them.

The choice of camera. This choice has, of course, been limited throughout the history of photography by the technology available at the time when a photographer was working. The main choices at the present time are among the hand-held 35mm and medium format (usually two-and-a-quarter-by-two-and-a-quarter-inch) cameras and the tripod-mounted view camera, which can take plates measuring up to eight by ten inches, or even larger. Some photographers, however, embrace the challenge of working with miniature cameras, antique cameras, Polaroid cameras, simple cameras designed for taking family snapshots, and even pinhole cameras.

The choice of film. The primary choice is between black-and-white and color film. If the photographer chooses black and white, then his secondary choices must determine the speed of the film (i.e., its sensitivity to light, which affects the length of time needed for proper exposure) as well as its graininess, its degree of contrast between light and dark tones, and its sensitivity to the relative values of colors.

The choice of subject. This choice is theoretically infinite, though throughout the history of photography it has been limited in practice by the sensibilities of individual photographers, by the prevailing taste of the time, and by the ability of the available technology to deal with certain kinds of subjects better than with others. The number of different photographs that can be made of any subject is also theoretically infinite, though it is limited in practice by judgment and economy.

The choice of environment. If the photographer has a choice, will he photograph the subject in his studio or elsewhere?

The choice of manipulation. Must the subject be photographed exactly as the photographer finds it, or may it be rearranged? Must the photographer refrain from intervening in an evolving situation or will he allow himself to stage a scenario as if he were a cinematic director?

The choice of how to frame the subject. Should the photographer shoot the subject close up or from far away? Should he isolate a detail or should he photograph the subject in context? If the latter, then what details of the environment should be included? From what angle should the subject be photographed, and what details should be most sharply in focus?

The choice of when to press the camera's shutter button. The British art critic John Berger has gone so far as to say that the crucial choice "is not between photographing x and y, but between photographing at x moment or at y moment."

The choice of lighting. In some cases, this is a variant of the choice of moment. In other cases, the choice is among using all natural light, all artificial light, or a combination of the two. If artificial light is to be used, will it be flash, flood or both?

The choice of lens. The photographer can, for instance, bring distant objects into close-up with a telephoto lens or greatly widen the field encompassed by the frame of the photograph with a wide-angle lens. Or he may use a telephoto lens simply to flatten out visual perspective in order to play tricks with spatial illusions.

The choice of filters. A yellow filter, for example, will make the sky much darker and the clouds much more clearly defined on black-and-white film than is possible with an unfiltered lens.

Beyond these variables, there are such factors as the availability of a desired subject, unexpected developments in the situation being photographed, and the photographer's luck, intelligence, sensitivity, reflexes, responsiveness to certain categories of subjects, and ability to improvise.

Furthermore, in addition to the variables that control the exposure of the film, there is another entire set of variables that is called into play in the processes of developing the negative and printing the image. Although in theory all prints from a single negative should be the same, in practice a highly trained eye may perceive differences among them—just as a discerning listener will be able to distinguish among various performances of a musical composition. Ansel Adams, who was a pianist before he turned to photography, put it well when he said, "The negative is the score; the print is the performance." This situation is complicated further when one photographer prints another's negatives, as when Berenice Abbott or Joel Snyder printed Atget's negatives. (Atget "restrikes" by both of those photographers are reproduced in this book.)

The choice of technique. Although the great majority of modern black-and-white prints are made with gelatin silver paper, some photographers prefer to make platinum prints, which are matte and which offer a subtler range of grays. Even within the standard range of silver papers there is a wide variation of levels of contrast. And then there is the whole spectrum of historical processes, including daguerreotypes, calotypes, tintypes, ambrotypes, albumen prints, carbon prints, and gum bichromate prints, each of which has its own particular look and mood, which greatly affect the impact of an image. Moreover, until black, white, and gray were accepted as the standard tonalities for monochromatic prints, photographers often printed their "black-and-white" work in tones that ranged—depending on the chemicals used—from warm browns, golds, reds, and purples to cool blues and greens. In looking at the pairs in this book, the reader should take into consideration that the plates are fairly uniformly sized halftone reproductions of black-and-white copy prints of original, vintage prints. As different as the reproductions within each pair may look, vintage prints hung side by side would differ even more—in color, degree of glossiness, size, and other respects.

The choice of print size. This choice affects both the clarity and the impact of an image. Although eight by ten inches has become the standard size for a black-and-white print, whether it be a contact print from a view-camera plate or an enlargement from a 35mm negative, contact prints can be as small as the inch-and-a-half-by-two-inch ones that André Kertész made in Paris in the early and middle 1920s or as large as the aptly named "mammoth" plates, measuring up to twenty-two by twenty-five inches that were used by many nineteenth-century photographer-explorers. The size of enlargements—which can cover entire walls—is virtually unlimited, although enlargements for exhibitions are usually printed on paper measuring either eleven by fourteen or sixteen by twenty inches.

The choice of whether or not to crop the negative. This is one of the most important choices in the entire process of making a photographic image. Some photographers regard their negatives simply as the raw material from which they can compose their images by cropping. They may even print numerous different images from a single negative by experimenting with various ways of cropping it. Other photographers adhere to the doctrine epitomized by Henri Cartier-Bresson, who has written, "If you start cutting or cropping a good photograph, it means death to the geometrically correct interplay of proportions. Besides, it very rarely happens that a photograph which was feebly composed can be saved by reconstruction of its composition under the darkroom's enlarger; the integrity of vision is no longer there."

The choice of chemicals and timing used in developing and printing. These choices make prints darker or lighter, more or less contrasty, warmly or coolly toned, matte or glossy.

The choice of whether or not to manipulate the print. The photographer can burn in areas that were underexposed or dodge areas that were overexposed. He can also solarize the print by exposing it to light while it is still developing, thereby achieving a partial reversal of lights and darks. Or he can sandwich negatives to make surrealistic combination prints, and so on *ad infinitum.*

The way a photographer resolves each of these technical decisions will reveal some facet of his artistic personality and intentions—but technical proficiency alone can never make a great photograph. Mastery of technique is essential insofar as it allows the photographer to express himself as fully as possible. He must, however, have something to say photographically.

Every great photograph is an ineffable blend of form and content, of technique and expression. As in writing, a photographic idea is inseparable from the form of its expression. Neither a writer nor a photographer can know *precisely* what he is trying to say until he has actually said it.

In photography, the process of working from general idea to specific expression can be a matter of finding a promising situation and then waiting and watching for the decisive moment—refining the event down to its essence and making a single perfect exposure. Or it can involve making many exposures and then zeroing in on the best one on the contact sheet. Some photographers feel that the negative must fully express the polished idea, while for others the printing and reprinting of the negative is like writing successive drafts of a manuscript. For them the photographic idea emerges fully only when they have made a perfect print.

THE COHERENCE OF A PHOTOGRAPHER'S STYLE

Even if one agrees that the photographer's compositional and technical decisions constitute expressive gestures, it still may seem that the style in which the forms and details of the subject are "drawn" in a photograph has more to do with the universal style of the camera itself or with the literal appearance of the subject than with the sensibility or talent of the photographer. It seems likely that many people would more or less assume that if a master photographer and a novice were photographing side by side, both could conceivably record the same details of the scene before them with the same degree of realistic accuracy. There would probably be nothing like the extreme difference that there would almost certainly be if a great painter and a novice worked side by side. The camera appears to be, in some respects, an artistic leveler and neutralizer. To what extent, then, are we justified in speaking of a distinctive style unifying any photographer's entire oeuvre?

In her brilliant and highly controversial book *On Photography,* Susan Sontag states that unless a photographer cultivates a formal mannerism or a thematic obsession throughout his career, his body of work will not have "the same integrity as does comparably varied work in other art forms." To make her point, she cites the example of Eadweard Muybridge, of whom she says:

> [T]here is no internal evidence for identifying as the work of a single photographer (indeed, one of the most interesting and original of photographers) those studies of human and animal motion, the documents brought back from photo-expeditions in Central America, the government-sponsored camera surveys of Alaska and Yosemite, and the "Clouds" and "Trees" series. Even after knowing that they were all

Carleton Watkins,
El Capitan, Yosemite, before 1866.
Albumen print. 20¾ x 15⅝.
NYPL.

taken by Muybridge, one still can't relate these series of pictures to each other (though each series has a coherent, recognizable style).

It is easy to understand how someone looking at Muybridge's work in isolation could find the various series disjointed. By comparing Muybridge's early Yosemite views with those of Carleton Watkins, however, one can more easily begin to identify the distinctive qualities that run throughout Muybridge's work.

When Carleton Watkins published his Yosemite views in San Francisco in 1867, they created such a sensation that Muybridge, a bookseller who avidly photographed the life of that city, decided to make a competing set of views. Through some combination of the photographer's temperament and strategy, Muybridge's views tend to be much more self-consciously dramatic than Watkins's—especially in regard to effects of light and shadow, to precarious or eccentric points of view, and to the use of natural forms as semi-abstract shapes within his photographic compositions.

These qualities become evident in Muybridge's view of El Capitan when we compare it with Watkins's much more classically composed and formally integrated photograph of the same subject. Watkins oriented his mammoth plate vertically to emphasize the upward sweep of the 3,600-foot-high, sheer rock face, and he composed his image so that the profile of the massive formation is more or less centered. Although Watkins stressed the grandeur of the cliff, he photographed it at a time when the light was so even that the textures and tonal values on the rock face are practically the same as those on the more distant mountains. Consequently, his photograph seems to make the point that although El Capitan is spectacular, it is an entirely natural part of the landscape—all of which is magnificent.

Muybridge, on the other hand, photographed El Capitan as a freak of nature. He used a horizontal composition, in which the cliff edge is well to the left of center, to emphasize not only the formation's height but also its breadth; and he dramatized that broad expanse of rock with bold highlights and shadows that throw the textures of the rock into high relief and isolate the giant rock from its surroundings. In contrast to the liveliness of the rock surface, the mountains in the background seem pale and insignificant, while the dark trees in the foreground—which, due to Muybridge's lower and closer viewpoint, appear to loom much taller than they do in the Watkins—establish an ominous barrier and provide a foil for the brilliant spectacle

Eadweard Muybridge,
El Capitan, Yosemite, 1867.
Albumen print. 5 x 8.
UCB.

behind them. In some prints of this image, Muybridge heightened the drama even further by printing lowering clouds from another negative in the narrow band of sky above the top of El Capitan.

All of the formal differences between Muybridge and Watkins would remain rather academic if they didn't point to something more than a personal rivalry that led the former to try to upstage the latter. But, as Weston Naef has argued in his definitive book on the nineteenth-century photographers of the American West, the stylistic differences between Muybridge's work and Watkins's had their roots in the philosophical positions of the two men:

> [B]y 1867 Muybridge and Watkins were working from substantially different artistic premises. Muybridge was very much the mannered romanticist, while Watkins was the essential classicist, eschewing visual gimmickry and opting to express as directly as possible his profound experience of nature. . . . Watkins idealized nature, treating it as the embodiment of a divine perfection, while for Muybridge nature was a series of juxtaposed paradoxes.

The consistency of the photographers' styles becomes apparent if we compare their photographs of Mirror Lake in Yosemite with each other and with their views of El Capitan. Watkins's image of Mirror Lake, dating from around 1861, is, like that of

El Capitan of about five years later, vertically composed. The highest point of the central mountain (which is El Capitan seen from behind) and the lowest point of its reflection are placed just slightly to the right of the central vertical axis of the photograph, dividing the picture laterally into two halves in which the profiles of the mountains and valleys very roughly echo one another. This symmetry approximates the much more obvious symmetry of the upper and lower halves of the picture, which are divided by the white streak of beach that lies just below the central horizontal axis. Watkins has composed his photograph like a balance whose equally weighted pans will never quite stop their up-and-down movement.

In his 1867 photograph of the same subject, Muybridge again, as in his photograph of El Capitan, used a horizontal format; and, with typically manneristic drama, he focused directly on the still water of the lake, recording only the reflected image of the mountain. To heighten the drama, he practically overwhelmed the pale reflection at the left with the dark reflection of the rock face at the right. Only the sliver of ground and the clumps of wildflowers at the bottom of the image help the viewer to get his bearings in this radically disorienting photograph.

Carleton Watkins,
Mirror Lake, Yosemite, c. 1861.
Albumen print. 20⅝ x 15¾.
Courtesy Lunn Gallery.

Eadweard Muybridge,
Mirror Lake, Yosemite, 1867.
Albumen print. 5 x 8. UCB.

By 1872, when Muybridge returned to Mirror Lake, he had become a virtuoso of sophisticated pictorial effects. He framed the left half of the picture almost exactly as Watkins had framed his, but he extended his image far to the right with a horizontal format. The rock face that looms at the right and the trees that span the middle of the photograph work together to create a powerful, semi-abstract form that distracts the viewer's attention from the paler mountain and its reflection that, nevertheless, subtly dominate the image. His photo is thus filled with especially great tensions between representation and abstraction.

Muybridge carried the attitudes and formal

mannerisms that he had begun to cultivate in Yosemite in 1867 directly over into the photographs of the Pacific coast and Alaska that he made the following year. He photographed many Alaskan towns from across bodies of water, just as he had composed many photographs in Yosemite.

Muybridge's studies of clouds dating from around 1869 can also be related through internal evidence to the Yosemite views in which he printed clouds from a separate negative. The glass plates used by Muybridge and Watkins were so highly sensitive to the blue light of the sky that the long exposures needed for landscape work left the skies a blank, overexposed white. If one made an exposure short enough to record clouds, the landscape would come out virtually black and without detail. During the 1860s, Watkins usually made no effort to compensate for the effect, but Muybridge was not willing to accept the limitations of his medium. Although today we take cloud-filled skies in landscape photographs for granted, a nineteenth-century viewer would have regarded a photograph in which both the landscape and the clouds were well defined as a *tour de force.* In the 1850s the challenge had been taken up by Roger Fenton in England and Gustave Le Gray in France, but both men had had to choose between sacrificing landscape detail for definition in the clouds or printing the landscape and the clouds from separate negatives, as Muybridge did.

It seems natural enough that Muybridge would have become interested in his negatives of clouds as images in their own right—not only because clouds were associated with dramatic virtuosity in photography but also because cloud studies formed an important category in the work of the landscape painters whose canvases Muybridge saw in San Francisco. Muybridge's cloud studies, in which no landscape at all appears, were the first in a long tradition that includes photographs by Alfred Stieglitz (his *Equivalent* series), Edward Weston, and Ralph Steiner.

In the late 1860s, Muybridge became so obsessed with photographing landscapes and clouds on single negatives that he invented a wooden shutter that could be opened and closed in front of the lens to diminish the amount of light reaching the plate directly from the sky. Such a reduction allowed him to balance the exposures from the landscape and the cloud-filled sky. He used this innovation dramatically in many of the photographs in his 1872 series of Yosemite, which created a sensation in San Francisco and throughout the United States.

It was certainly his virtuosity in recording the ephemeral that at least partially prompted Leland Stanford, a former governor of California, to ask Muybridge to help him settle a wager. In 1872 Stanford bet a friend $25,000 that at some point in its gallop a horse had all four of its legs off the ground at once. Since human vision is not fast enough to analyze such rapid movements, Stanford and his friend agreed that only a high-speed camera could serve as a reliable witness and resolve the dispute. Muybridge eventually made the necessary photographs by setting up a series of cameras whose shutters were tripped by threads stretched across a track. The photographs showed that at one point the horse did, indeed, have all four feet off the ground—but bunched together under his body, not stretched out hobbyhorse fashion, as painters until then had conventionally represented running horses.

In 1874, while still experimenting with methods of photographing Stanford's running horse, Muybridge discovered that his wife had a lover. He shot and killed him, and—in the spirit of the time—he was acquitted of his "crime of passion." Muybridge left the country in 1875 and traveled for a year in Central America. The photographs he made there of Indians in the jungles continue some of the concerns of the Yosemite and Alaskan views—namely, aquatic foregrounds and dramatic plays of light. In his photographs of Central American cities, Muybridge revived the photojournalistic interest in urban life that had characterized his earlier pictures of San Francisco.

As for the series of trees that Sontag mentions, it seems likely that she was thinking of an extended and important series by Watkins. Muybridge is not known to have made any such series.

When we study Muybridge's entire oeuvre and relate it to his personal history and to photographs by his contemporaries, we can see that his life's work developed coherently and logically as that of an artist in any other medium. To perceive that logic fully, one must be able to look at photographs abstractly, in terms of their purely formal qualities, as well as literally, in terms of the identity of their subjects. If one looks at photographs as if they were nothing more than literal records of the appearances of their subjects, the formal qualities that unite a photographer's entire body of work will never become evident, and all photographs of a particular subject—even when they are by photographers with widely differing styles—will always look more alike than different.

In spite of this general coherence, not every photograph will be a classic example of its maker's style, and, in fact, once one becomes familiar with a photographer's work, the anomalies may become as interesting as the classics. Much of the interest of any photograph lies in its relationship to the body of work to which it belongs. A knowledgeable viewer has the pleasure of perceiving how a specific photograph conforms to its photographer's style or varies from it. The farther a photograph is from the photographer's usual range of subject matter and style, the more interesting becomes the question, "Why did the photographer choose to photograph this particular subject and in this particular way?"

THE RELATIONSHIP BETWEEN STYLE AND SUBJECT MATTER

At any particular point in history, every category of subject matter seems to dictate a relatively narrow range of styles appropriate to its depiction, and, in turn, every style seems to dictate a relatively narrow range of appropriate subjects. This deep interrelationship between styles and subjects is evident not only in the history of photography but also in the history of painting. For example, virtually every stylistic breakthrough of the nineteenth century was tied to a narrow and specific range of subject matter. Think of the Realism of Daumier, Courbet, and Millet and their depictions of the poor, or think of Impressionism and the landscape along the Seine northwest of Paris. Or, continuing into the twentieth century, think of the succession of styles and their related subjects in Picasso's work: the old, blind, poverty-stricken people of the Blue Period; the women at their toilettes and the harlequins of the Rose Period; the figures playing musical instruments in Analytical Cubism; the still lifes of musical instruments, newspapers, and bottles in Synthetic Cubism; the minotaurs of the Surrealist Period. In Synthetic Cubism, the parallel planes of guitars and violins, the printed words of newspapers, and the transparency of bottles were so essential for the expression of Picasso's formal ideas that when Braque and Gris followed his lead, they had to adopt his subjects as well as closely related, though distinctive, formal styles.

One could write a history of photography strictly in terms of changing conceptions of what were technically possible and artistically worthy subjects for the camera. Such a history would show that as increasingly light-sensitive photographic emulsions were developed, the resulting reduction of exposure times allowed photographers to capture more and more ephemeral gestures and phenomena. During the 1880s, shorter exposures, the transition from heavy glass plates to small plates and then to lightweight cellulose film, and the manufacture of small cameras permitted photographers for the first time to dispense with the cumbersome tripods that had until then been required to keep their cameras steady during long exposures. From then on, the smaller and lighter that hand-held cameras became, the greater were their flexibility and range of potential subjects.

A history relating subject matter to technique would also have to take into consideration that the printing process most easily available during a given historical period greatly influenced the choice of subjects. The soft, middle gray tones of the platinum prints that were popular between about 1880 and the early 1920s, for example, encouraged photographers to choose subjects without strong contrasts of light and dark—such as softly lighted faces and landscapes. Some modern gelatin silver papers, on the other hand, can eliminate middle tones altogether, suiting them best to semi-abstract patterns formed by brilliant sunlight and dark shadows.

In terms of taste, the history of photography is largely a matter of extending the range of subjects and styles acceptable in photographs that are to be taken seriously as art—whatever their other functions may be. In general, one might note that the subjects chosen by nineteenth-century photographers tended to be famous, spectacular, bizarre, painterly, historically important, exotic, beautiful, distant, or otherwise intrinsically remarkable, while twentieth-century photographers have focused increasingly on subjects that are banal in themselves and thus present a challenge to the photographer who sets out to make a photograph that will be a work of art. The general history of style reflects the transition from the nineteenth-century assumption of photography's objectivity to the frank acknowledgment of its subjectivity in the twentieth century.

The one subject that has cut across all stylistic and technical boundaries from the time of photography's invention to the present day is the human face. Indeed, if one could imagine a survey of all photographs ever made, snapshot and studio portraits would probably overwhelm all other categories of images. Among photographers of the very greatest stature, only Atget comes readily to mind as one with no apparent interest in portraiture, though he photographed Paris and its environs with the attitude of a portraitist.

One could easily compile an entire book—and a fascinating one at that—containing nothing but comparisons of portraits of famous people by various photographers: Colette by Henri Cartier-Bresson and Irving Penn, James Joyce by Berenice Abbott and Gisèle Freund. Since, however, pairs of portraits of famous people do not raise questions of influence and coincidence to the same extent that other pairs do, no dual portraits of the same person have been included in this book.

COINCIDENCE, INFLUENCE, AND ORIGINALITY IN PHOTOGRAPHY

It is singularly appropriate that the history of photography should be punctuated with instances in which photographers have coincidentally focused on identical or similar subjects, for photography itself was invented independently and simultaneously, during the 1830s, by two men, one in France and one in England.

When Louis Jacques Mandé Daguerre's perfection of a photographic process was announced in Paris in January 1839, the news greatly distressed William Henry Fox Talbot, an Englishman who had first succeeded in making photographic images with a camera as early as 1835. Talbot, who was independently wealthy, had felt no pressing need to make public his invention or to exploit it commercially before Daguerre's announcement. Only the fear of losing the credit—and, to some extent, the income—due him as the first inventor of photography led him, within a matter of days after the news arrived from Paris, to exhibit samples of his own work. Nevertheless, the publicity attending Daguerre's announcement, as well as the superior clarity of his images, established the Frenchman in the popular imagination as the true inventor of photography.

In truth, it was Talbot's process, not Daguerre's, that provided the negative/positive principle on which modern photography is based. The daguerreotype process did not involve a negative; the positive image appeared directly on the copper plate. Consequently, a daguerreotype was a unique image that could not be reproduced except by being rephotographed. In Talbot's process, a negative image was formed when a sheet of paper treated with silver halides was exposed to light and then developed. After the negative had been oiled or waxed to make it translucent, it was placed in contact with another sheet of treated paper and exposed to light, producing a positive image. Since the paper negative slightly diffused the light that passed through it, Talbot's photographs, though highly detailed, had a softer quality than did Daguerre's. Thus, although we may say that Daguerre and Talbot invented photography independently and simultaneously, their inventions were actually very different from each other in technique and in the appearance of the final images.

In the history of science there are many examples of independent and more or less simultaneous discoveries—for example, Leibniz's invention of the infinitesimal calculus in 1684, three years before Newton published the slightly different system that he had begun to develop around 1665, or Alfred Wallace's arrival, in 1848, at a theory of evolution essentially identical to that which Darwin had conceived in 1842 but had not published. One could cite hundreds of other almost equally dramatic coincidences where various scientists picked up on problems and clues to their solutions that were "in the air" at the time. In an article on the role of geniuses in science, one authority has stated that "far from being odd or curious or remarkable, the pattern of independent multiple discoveries in science is in principle the dominant pattern, rather than a subsidiary one." In fact, practically all major discoveries in science are made at one time or another by at least two scientists who are unaware of each other's work. Similarly, in photography, if one searched long enough, one could probably find a double—in terms of subject or composition or both—for just about every photograph ever made.

If two scientists learn that they are both pursuing the same line of experiments, the less advanced will usually yield to the one who has proceeded further—unless he decides to race his more advanced colleague to the solution. Since discoveries in science are normally universally applicable solutions to objective problems, a proposed solution is either right or wrong, and the publication of a correct solution obviates the need for further research. The same is true in technology, where an invention either works or it doesn't—though it always remains subject to improvement.

The same is *not* true in photography, since every photograph is only a subjective solution to the unique problems confronting a specific photographer at the time he made a specific photograph. No photograph, however great it may be, can stand as the "correct" solution to the general problem of how to photograph a particular subject. If another photographer comes along to photograph the same subject, he will start afresh, except that he will probably try to avoid duplicating any previous pictures of the subject if he is aware of their existence.

Occasionally, despite the premium placed on originality in Western art, a photographer may decide to try to duplicate someone else's photograph more or less exactly. He may do this in a spirit of homage, or, if he is a young photographer, he may do it to develop his sense of kinship with the greats and to use their accomplishments as springboards for his own vision.

On a level considerably above intentions of mere duplication, a photographer might return to the subject of a famous photograph in a spirit of competition, certain that he can make a better photograph than his predecessor did. This attitude can lead either to inspired transformations or to displays of self-conscious cleverness, forced mannerisms, and pretentious artiness.

Alternatively, a photographer might seek out the subject of a photograph that interests him—or he might photograph a similar subject or composition—in order to enrich his own image with an allusion to its antecedent. He might think of his photograph as representing a move in the serious game of photography-as-art, in which new moves are accepted most readily if they make clever allusions to previously accepted works. The catch, of course, is that if a new work is *too* close to older works, it will be rejected by the most sophisticated members of the art audience. If, however, the allusion is subtle enough, it will provide a pleasurable thrill of recognition and sense of continuity for knowledgeable viewers.

A photographer may also be impressed by an image and then, after a while, forget that he has seen it. The image will, nevertheless, remain in his unconscious, so that it may eventually influence his choice and handling of subject matter—without his realizing that he is being influenced.

Most of the examples of approximate duplication in this book were probably created unintentionally. If the photographs here had been taken by amateurs totally unfamiliar with the traditions of photography and with the movements current at the time when they worked, then we would have to attribute these instances of unconscious duplication or similarity to pure chance. But all of the photographers represented here were or are highly sophisticated—so much so that we may speculate that if they did not actually know the earlier or contemporary photographs that they approximated, they were probably responding, when they made their own pictures, to cultural and aesthetic stimuli very similar to those that influenced their predecessors or contemporaries. In almost sixty percent of the pairs in this book, both photographs were made within ten years of each other, and in another fifteen percent they were made within twenty years. Coincidences within such short time spans seem almost inevitable in view of the speed and thoroughness with which, since about 1890, avant-garde publications, then art periodicals, magazines of all sorts, newspapers, books, and finally television have disseminated artistic ideas and styles.

Whether or not he has been influenced, every photographer legitimately claims every image he makes as uniquely his own. After all, even the acceptance of certain influences and the rejection of others is determined by—and revealing of—the photographer's background, circumstances, temperament, sensibility, and self-awareness. Each viewer must decide for himself exactly how interesting he finds the claim that the photographer has staked, at which point the subjectivity of the viewer's taste and his knowledge of the history of photography come into play.

The choice of subject matter, even if it has already been exploited by someone else, is a statement of personal vision at a given moment, whether the tangible result of that vision strikes the viewer as innocent, calculated, trite, or revelatory. One sure sign of genius is the talent for giving new life to subjects, styles, and ideas that everyone else thought were exhausted. It is, in fact, precisely this revivifying spark that we seek most assiduously when we look at art. Doing something passionately can count for much more than simply doing it first—although real innovation, however crude, is never without a certain passionate brilliance.

In one of his letters to his mistress, Gustave Flaubert wrote, "I think the greatest characteristic of genius is, above all, *power.* Hence, what I detest most of all in the arts, what sets me on edge, is the *ingenious,* the clever." What makes a photograph powerful is the sense it gives the viewer that the photographer cared passionately and intensely about his subject, about the way that he and his camera saw it, and about every detail of the final image. The viewer must sense that it was absolutely essential for the photographer to make that photograph in order to express some fundamental need. The basic, if self-evident, difference between an artist and other people is simply that an artist has a more highly developed sense of the *importance* and *urgency* of making art. Others may look at something and think, "That's interesting. It would make a nice photograph." But they will walk away without the photograph and—this is the crucial difference—without any profound sense of loss.

On the highest level originality itself—like the works of art that it produces—is ambiguous. It combines intuition and analysis; passion and a self-aware, distancing perspective; spontaneity and self-consciousness; and obsession and intelligence in such a way that the viewer cannot tell whether the resulting balance is tranquil or filled with extreme but equal tensions pulling in opposite directions. On the other hand, for those who are willing to look closely enough, *every* photograph, like every other work of art, is inevitably original. Any two people will always and unavoidably photograph the same subject differently, since they will see it and respond to it differently. Even two photographs of the same subject by the same person will differ, since any alteration in the subject or change in the light or shift in the photographer's position or mood will yield a different picture.

At the opening of an exhibition of his work at the Royal Photographic Society in 1900, the great English architectural photographer Frederick H. Evans spoke of this extreme sensitivity of photography. "I have often tried to repeat certain negatives," he said, speaking of negatives that he himself had made earlier, "but have invariably failed, most so of course in out-of-door work: but even in interiors I think I might challenge any one to go to any of my subjects on these walls and bring away an exact replica, in print as well as in negative of course: he may do better (or worse), but to repeat it with the so-called mechanical accuracy of the box with a glass in it, I say, is impossible, and if this does not mean individuality it means nothing, and individuality is the basis of all art."

Visual artists and their public have much to learn about the nature and perception of originality from performers of classical music. Nobody would berate a musician for playing a composition that has been played frequently before, and, indeed, the vast majority of concerts in Europe and the United States consist of familiar pieces. The musical audience accepts this state of affairs—indeed, demands it by being generally inhospitable to new compositions—and is prepared to listen closely to hear the nuances that distinguish a particular performance of a piece from all other performances of it. The members of the audience listen both for the pleasure of hearing again music that they love and for the pleasure of hearing a great performer make the music his own through the subtleties and passion of his interpretation.

It is the transformative, renewing power of the photographer's unique and passionate vision that, in the end, is the most important element in any great photograph. If the photographer brings to his work intelligence and genuine passion for making photographs, as well as openness to the unexpected and an ability to look intensely and imaginatively at the world, then his photographs—regardless of the intrinsic interest or banality of their subjects and regardless of whether his photographs are straight, staged, manipulated, or whatever—can hardly help being powerful and full of a life of their own.

The young photographer and the amateur (or even the mature professional, for that matter) should never be discouraged just because somebody tells him that his idea isn't new. Since every photograph is both a depiction of its nominal subject and an oblique self-portrait of the photographer, the character and intelligence that we see reflected in the image can transform the most hackneyed subject matter. It is as if the act of framing the subject in the viewfinder of the camera—of isolating the subject and focusing on it—charges the photograph with the photographer's energy. We feel the power of the photographer's eye, reflected in the photograph almost as if it were the source of light.

PHOTOGRAPHS & COMMENTARIES

10

In 1844 Talbot chose *The Haystack* for inclusion in *The Pencil of Nature,* the first photographic book ever published, because the image so dramatically demonstrates the camera's ability to record "a multitude of minute details" and "every accident of light and shade." But *The Haystack* is far more than just a technical *tour de force* for its time; it is an extraordinarily bold and mysterious photograph. The sculptured haystack, whose forms and surface textures are wonderfully articulated by highlights and shadows, looks like an enchanted thatched cottage in a forest clearing. The ladder, together with its shadow, serves as a strong compositional device, as a metaphor for photography (the shadow representing the negative image of the ladder "written" with light on the side of the haystack), and perhaps also as a symbol of the upward progress of science.

Regnault, who, like Talbot, was a prominent scientist, had almost certainly seen

The Haystack by the time he made his photograph of a ladder. Regnault would probably have seen a copy of Talbot's book when, about 1847, he assisted Louis-Désiré Blanquart-Evrard, who later became an important photographic publisher, in his experiments to improve Talbot's calotype process. Moreover, Regnault was a friend of the family of Sir John Herschel, who was one of Talbot's closest friends.

Regnault, whose photograph was published by Blanquart-Evrard in 1853, may have derived his basic composition from Talbot. The placement of the ladder and the shape of the stucco wall are certainly reminiscent of *The Haystack*. But the similarity ends there. Regnault's photograph is as delightfully cluttered as Talbot's is spare, and the space defined by the parallel, perpendicular, and obstructing walls in the Regnault is as complex and ambiguous as that of a Cubist painting. *(See notes on photogenic drawings, calotypes, and Blanquart-Evrard's calotype process.)*

Victor Regnault,
Untitled (A Ladder),
before 1853.
Salt print. 8 x 11.
Private collection.

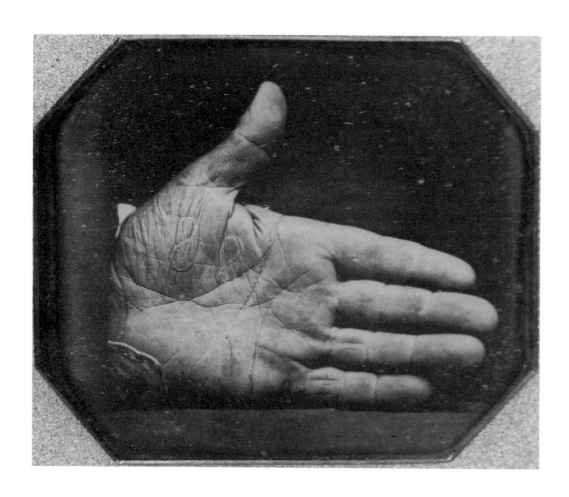

Albert Sands Southworth and Josiah Johnson Hawes, *Captain Jonathan W. Walker's Branded Hand,* 1845. Daguerreotype. 2³/₄ x 3¹/₄. MHS, Bowditch Coll.

Southworth and Hawes's brutally direct image makes Captain Walker's hand seem almost severed from his body—like a grisly piece of evidence. And, in fact, the daguerreotype does provide chilling evidence of crime and punishment—though the punishment turns out to have been far more criminal than the "crime." On Walker's right hand, just below his thumb, are clearly visible the letters *SS,* standing for "slave stealer." (Like all daguerreotypes made without correcting lenses, the image is laterally reversed, making Walker's hand appear to be his left and making the letters read backward.) In 1844 Walker had been caught while sailing seven escaped slaves from Florida to freedom in the West Indies. After a year in prison and the ordeal of branding, he became an ardent crusader for abolition. Southworth and Hawes, who photographed many distinguished abolitionists, were clearly sympathetic to the cause.

Although sketches of hands are common in the history of art, the tradition of letting images of hands represent an individual's personality is largely a photo-

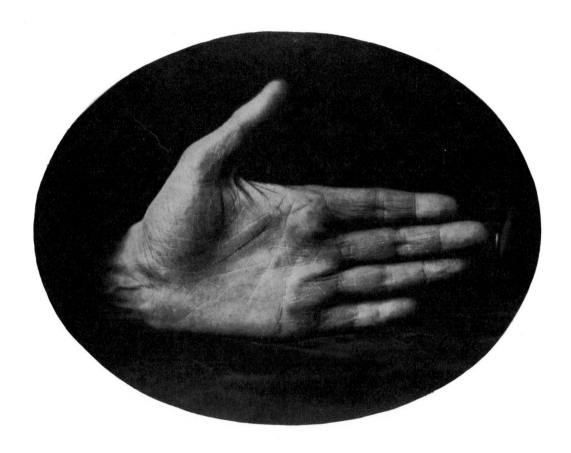

graphic one. The earliest photograph of an isolated hand was made by Talbot in 1841. Ever since then, hands—particularly those of artists and writers—have been popular subjects. One could cite, for example, Berenice Abbott's photograph of Cocteau's hands and Strand's of Braque's.

In 1853 Charles Hugo made a famous photograph of the hand of his father, Victor, the great writer who was a friend of Nadar's. That photograph may well have inspired Nadar—in many of whose best portraits the sitters' hands are almost as expressive as their faces—to make this unusual "portrait" of Monsieur D. . . . , an anonymous banker. In contrast to the Southworth and Hawes image, which he could not have seen, Nadar's photograph is an elegant picture of a refined hand with long, tapering fingers. The oval format suggests a painted miniature, while the velvet on which the hand rests may have been the studio cloak in which Sarah Bernhardt and George Sand wrapped themselves for their Nadar portraits. *(See notes on daguerreotypes and albumen prints.)*

Nadar,
The Left Hand of Monsieur D . . . , A Banker, c. 1860. Albumen print (printed by electric light). 6 x 7^1/$_2$. Courtesy Harry N. Abrams, Inc. and SFP.

Edouard-Denis Baldus,
*The Chapel of the Holy Cross
at Montmajour,* 1849.
Salt print. 13 3/16 x 17.
Coll. Phyllis Lambert,
on loan to CCA.

The Chapel of the Holy Cross at Montmajour is the earliest known photograph by Baldus, and yet it is a splendid example of his mature style. Baldus frequently photographed his subjects from a distance in order to show them in their contexts, and he often chose oblique points of view both to convey a sense of volume and to add to the drama of his compositions. To heighten this drama further, he favored large formats (up to seventeen and one-half by twenty-three inches); and to provide the climax for the drama, Baldus repeatedly composed his photographs so that the highest point of the subject would almost touch the top edge of the image.

In May 1852, Baldus published a thirty-two-page book describing his project of photographing the principal historic monuments of the Midi, the area of central France in which Montmajour is located. This book probably inspired Nègre's trip to photograph the Midi, beginning in August 1852. Nègre could perhaps have met

Charles Nègre,
The Chapel of the Holy Cross at Montmajour, 1852.
Salt print 12⁹/₁₆ x 8³/₄.
Coll. André Jammes, Paris.

Baldus and seen his work through Henri Le Secq, who was one of Nègre's closest friends and who, like Baldus, photographed for the Commission des Monuments Historiques in 1851. Baldus himself returned to the Midi in 1852.

Baldus photographed the church as a work of architecture in a landscape. Nègre, however, set up his camera so close to the central forms of the church—but along the same axis of vision as Baldus—that he eliminated all suggestion of the surrounding landscape and even cut off much of the church, making the building look like a work of sculpture. Nègre emphasized the plasticity of the church's forms through lighting as dramatic as that in Talbot's *Haystack (see page 40).* The sculptural massiveness implied by the way the forms fill the image surface makes Nègre's photograph remarkably similar to Ansel Adams's of the church at Ranchos de Taos *(see page 118).*

An 1848 engraving of the view of lower Manhattan from the steeple of Saint Paul's Church clearly shows Brady's Daguerrean Miniature Gallery on the top floor of the building at the southwest corner of Broadway and Fulton Street, while Barnum's Museum was one block to the north. Barnum, whose "museum" housed an extensive collection of freaks, took full advantage of the nearness of Brady's studio by having Brady make publicity portraits of his star attractions.

Brady's portrait of a woman almost eight feet tall and a man barely three feet tall simultaneously emphasizes and denies the abnormality of the subjects. Although the pose establishes their relative heights, one might guess—if one didn't have information to the contrary—that the woman was simply an imposing figure about six feet tall and that the midget was about two and a half feet tall.

Brady's photograph is also ambiguous in regard to the subjects' social position and relationship to each other. Brady has posed them, with the man's hand on the woman's shoulder, as if they were a normal and even distinguished married couple.

And yet the pose is also reminiscent of that conventionally used at the time for mothers and children. To some extent, however, the pose must have been purely practical; the man needed to steady himself on that high stool.

Atget, who had no way of knowing Brady's work, often photographed deserted streets. In fact when he photographed the streets of Paris, he usually began working at dawn in order to avoid people, who, if they moved, would have apeared as blurs in his images. It is, therefore, very much in character that Atget's hauntingly mysterious photograph of a sideshow juxtaposing a giant and a midget should not include the men themselves, but only their props and photographs of them. The photograph provides hardly a hint of context. Except for the pieces of paper that indicate the entrance fee as one franc, the display, emerging out of empty, black space, is suggestive of a bedroom bureau covered with photographs and bizarre knickknacks. Atget conveys the spontaneous and ambiguous poetry of the display so eloquently that photographing the men themselves would have been anticlimactic.

Eugène Atget,
*Fête du Trône,*1922–25.
Albumen print. 6½ x 8½.
MoMA, Abbott-Levy.

Charles Nègre,
A Fallen Horse, Paris, 1851.
Albumen print. $3^{1}/_{8}$ x $3^{5}/_{8}$.
Private collection.

Early in 1851 Nègre designed a combination of lenses that focused light onto the sensitized paper in his camera with greater intensity than did the conventional lenses of the day. This invention made possible much shorter exposure times and allowed Nègre to photograph people as they went about their activities in the streets of Paris. It is fitting that Nègre, who had been trained as a painter, introduced the painterly tradition of genre—scenes of everyday life—into photography.

Most of Nègre's genre photographs fall into one or the other of two categories—candid shots in which the subjects were moving too quickly for the camera to record them without some blurring and posed shots in which street tradespeople remained still while Nègre photographed them.

When a draft horse collapsed on the cobbled street outside Nègre's house on the Ile Saint-Louis in Paris, the photographer moved swiftly to record the incident. The result is one of his finest street photographs, for it combines the spontaneity of his candid shots with the clarity of his posed shots.

Kertész, who had not seen Nègre's photograph, made his image of a draft horse

that collapsed on a cobbled Paris street in 1927, the year before he bought his first 35mm camera. He had, however, used a small plate camera (making negatives approximately two inches by two and one-half inches) since he had begun photography in 1912. His camera was small and light enough so that he could hold it steady and at any angle in his hands rather than having to mount it on a tripod, as Nègre had had to do. This lightness gave Kertész great flexibility and versatility in his approaches to his subjects—allowing him, for instance, to photograph from above. By taking an overhead position, Kertész eliminated all the setting that gives the Nègre its charm. Kertész's photograph was aggressively modern for its time—and quite witty, since the overhead viewpoint playfully suggests that the horse is in a walking position against the background of a brick wall.

The subject was of long-standing interest to Kertész, for he had photographed a farm couple trying to raise their fallen horse on a country road in Hungary in 1916. Kertész's Parisian photograph is the first in a sequence of six in which the horse gets up and walks away.

André Kertész,
A Fallen Horse, Paris, 1927.
Gelatin silver print. 4 x 5¹/₂.
© André Kertész.

Philip Henry Delamotte,
*Scaffolding for the Erection
of the Great Ribs of the
Center Transept,
Crystal Palace* c. 1852.
Albumen print. 8 x 6.
Gernsheim Coll., HRC/UT.

The Crystal Palace—built in London for the Great Exhibition of 1851 and filled with all the latest inventions, including photographs—was one of the wonders of its age. It caused such a sensation that a group of businessmen decided to buy the structure, which was slated for demolition at the close of the exhibition, and move it to the London suburb of Sydenham. They hired Delamotte, a drawing teacher and an amateur photographer, to document the entire process of reconstruction, which lasted from 1851 to 1854. His brilliantly composed and detailed photographs, 160 of which were published by the owners of the Crystal Palace in two lavish volumes in 1855, constitute one of the first extensive photo-essays.

In 1923 the versatile Moholy-Nagy began teaching metalwork at the Bauhaus, the great school of architecture and industrial design founded in Weimar, Germany, in 1919 by the architect Walter Gropius. Since the Crystal Palace was such an important antecedent of Gropius's own glass-and-steel buildings, it seems quite possible that Delamotte's books might have found their way into the Bauhaus library, where Moholy-Nagy could have seen them. If Moholy-Nagy did see Delamotte's photo-

graph of scaffolding, he would certainly have been struck by the extraordinary modernity of its almost abstract composition.

When Moholy-Nagy traveled to Paris in 1925, a number of factors must have drawn him immediately to the Eiffel Tower. As a teacher of metalwork, he would have been interested in the world's most spectacular metal structure; as the traveling companion of Sigfried Giedion, a noted Swiss historian of modern architecture, he would have been aware of the tower's importance in the evolution of the Bauhaus aesthetic; and as a photographer interested in abstraction, he would have recognized the tower's potential for strongly patterned, disorienting compositions. In the dynamic, almost Futuristic photograph reproduced here, which resembles some of Moholy-Nagy's abstract, negative photograms of the period, it is difficult to get one's bearings. The spiral stairs running up the center and the apparent narrowing of the structure toward the center of the image indicate, however, that Moholy-Nagy was pointing his camera obliquely upward. Similarly, in the Delamotte, only the roof's curved glass sheathing, visible at the upper left, shows which way is up.

László Moholy-Nagy,
Eiffel Tower, 1925.
Gelatin silver print.
$11\frac{1}{2}$ x $8\frac{5}{8}$.
Larson Coll.
© William Larson.
Courtesy Hattula
Moholy-Nagy.

The Bisson brothers made their photograph when the facade of the cathedral was undergoing repairs. The scaffolding may have especially interested the Parisian photographers, since Notre-Dame de Paris had itself been covered with scaffolding from about 1845 to 1855, while Viollet-le-Duc's restorations were in progress.

The Bisson brothers set up their camera at sufficient distance from the cathedral to include a row of stone roadway markers that establishes a visual boundary between the viewer and the cathedral, which almost seems to be on a stage. The Alinari photograph, taken closer in, gives much more sense of the cathedral's being set in a landscape in which the viewer is present. The mountain that is just barely visible at the far right of the Alinari photograph, taken on a sunny day, enhances this sense of landscape.

The clear, soft, even lighting without distinct shadows makes it apparent that the

Bisson photograph was made on a bright overcast day—ideal conditions for highly detailed architectural photographs. The bright sunlight in the Alinari nicely highlights the rhythm of the facade columns, but it also casts deep shadows that obliterate many fine details.

The highlighted, domed structure at the far left of the Alinari distracts the eye away from the cathedral, thereby making the photograph considerably less effective and sensitive than that by the Bisson brothers, who have included just enough of that building to acknowledge its presence and to balance their composition. The Bisson brothers would almost certainly have known the Alinari image, since, by the late 1850s, they were selling Alinari photographs in their Parisian studio. Once they had made competing views, they presumably sold only their own. *(See note on Blanquart-Evrard's calotype process.)*

Bisson Frères,
Pisa Cathedral, 1860s.
Albumen print. 14 x 18.
Courtesy Sotheby's.

Charles Marville,
Rue des Sept Voies,
Paris, c. 1860.
Albumen print.
13³/₈ x 10¹/₄.
MC.

During the February Revolution of 1848, the insurrectionists threw up barricades across many of the narrow, labyrinthine streets of the medieval quarters of Paris, thereby impeding the movements of government troops. To prevent the recurrence of such tactics, Napoleon III ordered Baron Haussmann to widen the old streets and to demolish some old neighborhoods entirely to make way for broad—and easily policed—boulevards. In the 1850s and the 1860s, Haussmann employed Marville to make a comprehensive photographic record of the condemned areas.

Because the narrowness of the old streets prevented him from getting far enough back from individual houses to photograph their facades, Marville generally set up his camera so that it looked right down the middle of the street, taking in as much of both sides as possible. To photograph the rue des Sept Voies, looking toward the Pantheon, he stood where the street intersected the rue Saint-Hilaire and composed his picture vertically so that he could take in everything from the sign in the left foreground to the top of the Pantheon's dome. He also took in several people who appeared in their doorways and windows during the exposure.

When Atget went to the Musée Carnavalet (the museum of the history of Paris) to sell his prints, someone might have shown him Marville's work as an example of the kind of documentation they sought. But by the time Atget made his photograph of the rue Valette, as the rue des Sept Voies was renamed after it had been widened, he was no longer particularly interested in documentation. During the 1920s he returned to many of the streets he had photographed meticulously before World War I and made wonderfully soft and poetic images. Early one morning in March 1925, Atget set up his camera on the sidewalk of the widened street in order to focus on the intact old houses, as Marville had been unable to do. The angle also allowed him to avoid showing any more of the new buildings on the right than was absolutely necessary for the balance of his horizontal composition. The street is totally deserted, as Atget liked his streets to be.

In order to record details in the dark areas along the street, both photographers had to make such long exposures that the brightly lighted Pantheon was overexposed—making it seem to glow through a soft mist.

Eugène Atget,
Coin de la rue Valette et le Panthéon, 5e arrondissement, matinée de mars, 1925. Albumen print. 7 x 9½. MoMA/CAW.

Thomas Annan,
Close No. 157, Bridgegate,
Glasgow, 1868.
Carbon print. 11¼ x 8⅞.
Private collection.

In 1868 the Glasgow City Improvement Trust commissioned Annan, who was well known as a photographer of Glasgow architecture, to photograph the city's slums that were to be demolished in order to make way for wider streets and new buildings. The trustees wanted from Annan—as Baron Haussmann had wanted from Marville—a series of photographs that would serve as historical documentation of the old buildings, as a tool for social and sanitary workers, and as the "before" side of the before-and-after comparisons that would show how much had been accomplished by the demolition and reconstruction.

Like Marville, Annan had a thriving business photographing works of art. And also like Marville, Annan took his camera into old and overcrowded neighborhoods only because he was paid to do so. In this respect, Atget differed from both of his distinguished predecessors. He worked on his own initiative, choosing subjects that appealed to him for one reason or another. He photographed the Passage Vaudrezanne presumably because he found it "picturesque," which is to say that he sensed that he could make a satisfying picture of it. As a free-lance photographer, however,

Eugène Atget,
*Passage Vaudrezanne,
Butte-aux-Cailles, 13e arron-
dissement, Paris,* 1900.
Albumen print. $8^{1}/_{2}$ x $6^{3}/_{4}$.
MoMA, Abbott-Levy.

Atget also had to keep the needs of his customers in mind. His photographs had to appeal both to the artists and designers who used them as source materials and to the libraries and museums that bought them strictly on account of the interest of their subject matter rather than their beauty as photographs.

It is possible that when Atget made his rounds of prospective clients, someone showed him a copy of Annan's book *Photographs of Old Closes, Streets, &c.,* in which the photograph of Close No. 157 was included. The book had first been published, with beautiful carbon prints, in 1878–79 and reissued with photogravure plates in 1900, the year Atget photographed the Passage Vaudrezanne.

Although the compositions of the Annan and the Atget are remarkably similar, the narrowness of the passageway and of the patch of sky in the Atget, as well as the rise in the street countered by the flow of water in the gutter, makes the Atget, which dates from the very beginning of his grand survey of Paris, a more dynamic photograph than the hauntingly static Annan, over which hangs the calm before the storm of demolition. (*See note on carbon prints.*)

Annan's *Photographs of Old Closes, Streets, &c.* was the first book of photographs of slums ever published. Annan, who was always very concerned with the permanence of his photographic prints, had set up a plant for producing carbon prints, which are not susceptible to fading, in Lenzie, Scotland, where he had the prints for the book made from his negatives. Carbon prints, because of their grainless texture, their relatively matte surfaces, and their subtle gradations of tones, were favored for portraits and for reproductions of works of art. It is thus rather ironic that Annan chose the process for his photographs of slums. The picturesque sensibility that Annan brought to the Glasgow slums is especially evident in the photograph of Close No. 193, where the photographer has superimposed clouds onto what would otherwise have been a blank white sky.

Photographs of Old Closes, Streets, &c. was published in an edition of only one hundred copies, most of which were given to Glasgow officials. It is, therefore, unlikely that Riis could have seen Annan's book before the large photogravure edition of *Old Closes* appeared in 1900.

While Annan and Marville were commissioned to photograph condemned areas, Riis photographed so that he could persuade New York officials to condemn the worst slums and to provide better housing for the poor. Riis's photographs have special conviction, since, when he first arrived in New York as an immigrant from Denmark, he had been unable to find work and had had to live in the slums that he later photographed.

Unlike Annan, Riis wasn't primarily a photographer. He was a reporter, and, as far as he was concerned, the camera was simply a tool that enabled him to make powerful images of the poor. Also unlike Annan, Riis was primarily interested in people—especially children. Even in his photograph of Baxter Street Alley, in which he was ostensibly documenting the general look of the place, Riis clearly centered his attention on the two girls, who look as if their circumstances have forced them to a maturity beyond their years. In the Annan, by contrast, the two children appear as spectral, faceless blurs. Annan had been commissioned to photograph the closes, not the people who lived in them.

Jacob Riis,
Baxter Street at Mulberry Bend, New York, 1888. Modern gelatin silver print from original negative. 9¹/₄ x 7³/₈. MCNY.

William Henry Jackson,
Old Faithful Geyser,
Yellowstone, 1871.
Albumen print. 8¾ x 6¾.
Private collection.

Old Faithful's rushing, evanescent plume of steam and water was a subject nearly impossible for Jackson's slow, blue-light-sensitive, wet-collodion plates to record. In an exposure of normal length, the geyser would have been visible but blurred up to the dark horizon and invisible against the white sky. Therefore, Jackson used as short an exposure as possible and retouched the sky area of his negative by hand, blocking out some of the light so that the geyser would stand out clearly. To emphasize the geyser's height, Jackson posed some figures near its mouth.

Because of the technical difficulties involved, Jackson's photograph is not typical of the work of the man who later, on the title page of one of his books of Rocky Mountain scenery, billed himself as "the world's greatest photographic artist." Most of Jackson's Yellowstone photographs, which in 1872 persuaded Congress to declare the area the first national park, are carefully composed images of static formations. But Old Faithful was such an incredible spectacle that documenting it at all must have seemed more important than worrying about artistic finesse. It is now the very

crudeness and sense of discovery in the photograph that makes it so appealing to modern eyes.

Adams photographed Old Faithful for the first time in 1941, when he was photographing national parks for the Department of the Interior, and he returned to the subject several times during the 1940s. He must have known Jackson's photograph, for he included a number of Jacksons in the exhibition of photographs of the Civil War and the American frontier that he organized at the Museum of Modern Art in New York in 1942. Jackson, who was then ninety-nine years old, attended the opening of the exhibition.

In order to illuminate the geyser as brilliantly as possible, Jackson set up his camera so that the sun was behind him. But Adams shot toward the sun, which was partially obscured by clouds. His image of the dark, majestic, but rather wistful-looking geyser—which towers above the low cumulus clouds—is one of his most awesome and moving photographs.

Ansel Adams,
Old Faithful Geyser,
Yellowstone National Park,
1941.
Gelatin silver print.
9 x 6³/₈.
Courtesy the artist.

Timothy O'Sullivan,
Canyon de Chelly, 1873.
Albumen print. 10³/₄ x 8.
Courtesy Lunn Gallery.

In 1873, 1st Lt. George M. Wheeler, commander of the Army Corps of Engineers' Geological Surveys West of the Hundredth Meridian, delegated O'Sullivan to photograph Indians and archaeological ruins in northeastern Arizona. This photograph of the ancient cliff dwellings in the Canyon de Chelly, made on that expedition, is composed so that the entire surface of the image is packed with information. O'Sullivan photographed the scene in bright, clear light, and he included two figures on the upper ruins and two on the lower ones to establish scale.

About 1875, the Army Corps of Engineers published original prints of many of O'Sullivan's photographs in an album entitled *Photographs Showing Landscapes, Geological and Other Features of Portions of the Western Territory of the United States.* Ansel Adams not only knew this book but also owned a copy of it. When, in 1937, Beaumont Newhall asked Adams to send some of his own photographs for the Museum of Modern Art's landmark survey of the history of photography, Adams agreed and also offered to send the O'Sullivan book, of which he said. "A few

of the photographs are extraordinary—as fine as anything I have ever seen." Adams later wrote that O'Sullivan's photographs "opened a wide new world" for him and that the view of the Canyon de Chelly is "perhaps O'Sullivan's finest photograph . . . an image of great power and revelation."

If O'Sullivan had included a patch of sky in his photograph, as Adams did in his, it would have registered on his overly blue-light-sensitive plate as a distracting, blank, white shape. Adams, who has occasionally published his image with the sky cropped out, made his sky even darker than it would normally have appeared on his color-balanced film by using a yellow filter over his lens. The filter also accentuated the striations of the rock face.

O'Sullivan seems to have been primarily interested in showing the upper and lower ruins in their context, while Adams, who included no people and only the upper ruins in his photograph, seems to have been primarily interested in the dramatic upward sweep of the cliff.

Ansel Adams,
White House Ruin,
Canyon de Chelly
National Monument, c. 1942.
Gelatin silver print.
19 x 13³/₄.
Courtesy the artist.

Thomson was the first to publish a book of photographs of the poor. Soon after he returned to London in 1872, having spent ten years in Asia, Thomson began to photograph the laborers, tradespeople, and denizens of the streets of London—just as he had photographed their counterparts in China. He posed his subjects carefully but naturally, making sure that they did not move during the exposures. Perhaps because Thomson had been abroad for so long—and because the gulf between the English middle and lower classes was so broad—his photographs of humble Londoners look like the work of a sympathetic anthropologist from an alien culture.

Thomson was accompanied on his photographic exploration of the streets of London by the writer Adolphe Smith, who interviewed the people whom Thomson photographed. In 1877 they began to publish their collaborative book, *Street Life in London,* which appeared in twelve monthly installments with three small woodburytypes tipped into each. In their introduction, Thomson and Smith wrote that "the precision of photography . . . will enable us to present true types of the London Poor and shield us from accusations of either underrating or exaggerating individ-

ual peculiarities of appearance." Smith wrote of the photograph reproduced here that it was made on "a vacant piece of land at Battersea" and that the nomads "attend fairs, markets, and hawk cheap ornaments or useful wares from door to door."

It is intriguing to wonder whether Atget, who began his photographic career with a series on street tradespeople remarkably similar to Thomson's, might have seen a copy of Thomson's book at one of the libraries to which he sold prints. But even if Atget did get ideas for subject matter from Thomson, his poetic vision surpassed Thomson's. Because of the discrepancy of focus between the foreground and the background in Thomson's photograph, in which none of the people looks toward the camera, the subjects appear to be forming a *tableau vivant* in front of a painted backdrop. In Atget's photograph, everyone is looking at the camera—with a range of expressions from amusement to worry, resentment, and downright hostility—while the light between the vans is as sublime as the light in any of Turner's paintings. *(See note on woodburytypes.)*

Eugène Atget,
Porte de Choisy, 1914.
Albumen print.
$6^{3}/_{4}$ x $8^{15}/_{16}$.
MoMA, Abbott-Levy.

Count Giuseppe Primoli,
Widow in a Gondola,
Venice, c.1890.
Gelatin silver print.
7$\frac{1}{2}$ x 7$\frac{1}{8}$.
FP.

The invention in the 1870s of gelatin dry plates—which could be purchased ready to use, stored until needed, and processed commercially at leisure—gave rise to hordes of amateur photographers. The wet-collodion process that had prevailed until then was so messy and so demanding that few people other than professionals were willing to use it.

Primoli, a member of an aristocratic Italian family related to the Bonapartes, had the time and the money to pursue his photographic hobby with such a passion that between the late 1880s and 1900, he made over twenty thousand photographs. His subjects range from the court ceremonies and sporting pastimes of the nobility to spontaneous, and often amusing, snapshots of street life and of his friends, who included many of the greatest artists, writers, and theatrical personalities of his time.

It has been suggested that the woman in the gondola in the Primoli photograph was not really an anonymous widow at all, but rather the great actress Eleonora Duse, who was one of Primoli's closest friends. Primoli was certainly not above such deception, for he had a playful side and, much of the time, was out to have fun with

his camera. But whoever the beautiful woman really was, and whatever the circumstances under which the photograph was made, the image remains haunting and filled with mysterious silence. The poor condition of the negative increases the image's poignance and suggests that the photograph is a more ancient relic than it actually is.

Lange, who had probably never heard of Primoli, used the oval shape and the reflectiveness of the car window to make an ironic allusion to the soft-focus portraits that she had made before turning to documentary photography in the early 1930s. The oval window and the cabriolet brace suggest the sort of frame in which one might put a miniature portrait—and, indeed, the image of the woman's face, which is partially obscured by reflections of clouds in the bright sky, looks strikingly similar to the soft-focus portrait of a woman named Adele Raas that Lange made around 1920. The sharp focus of the automobile body, however, makes it clear that the blurriness was inherent in the situation, not imposed by the photographer's sensibility. *(See notes on gelatin dry plates and gelatin silver prints.)*

Dorothea Lange,
Funeral Cortege, End of an Era in a Small Valley Town, California, 1938.
Gelatin silver print.
9³/₁₆ x 7¹/₂.
OM.

Eugène Atget,
Sleeping Vagrant,
Paris, c. 1900.
Albumen print, 7 x 8½.
Courtesy Sotheby's.

Although one generally thinks of Atget as a photographer of deserted streets, he actually made many photographs of people—an extensive series on street vendors, a series on ragpickers *(see page 65),* a series on prostitutes, numerous street scenes with people, and even a picture of a group of people watching an eclipse. Atget, then, was no misanthropist. He just usually tried to keep people out of his architectural and topographical photographs.

Atget's photograph of a down-and-out man dates from soon after 1900, when he was making his series on street vendors—a category into which this sleeping derelict hardly fits. Atget may have regarded the man as a picturesque type without which his portrait of Paris would be incomplete, or he may have viewed him as a sympathetic character, as an interesting form, or simply as an enigma, since the man's face is covered by his hat and by something that looks like a tiny dog.

Moholy-Nagy, who was one of the principal organizers of the *Film und Foto* exhibition held in Stuttgart in 1929, probably first saw Atget's photographs during the preparations for the show, to which Berenice Abbott sent ten Atget prints. This

photograph of a vagrant was not among them. Moholy-Nagy had, in any case, already made his photograph of a similar subject.

Moholy-Nagy, who moved with ease from painting to photograms to camera images to films, made his photograph of a vagrant sleeping near the harbor of Marseilles while he was working on a film about the harbor: *Marseille Vieux Port.* The photograph is totally unexpected in Moholy-Nagy's predominantly playful, formalistic oeuvre, for it comes closer than almost anything else done in Europe at that time to the style that would be developed by the photographers working for the Resettlement Administration in the 1930s. Moholy-Nagy's eloquent and deeply affecting photograph is neither sentimental nor tendentious.

Atget has shown the man totally sealed off in a world of his own. Indeed, the ground and the wall form such a neutral, continuous background that the man almost appears to be floating in space. In the Moholy-Nagy, the strong perspective of the wall on the left pulls the viewer's eye from the sleeping man into the sunlit world of shops and motorcars.

László Moholy-Nagy,
Sleeping Vagrant,
Marseilles, 1929.
Gelatin silver print.
8 x 12$\frac{1}{2}$.
Courtesy Sotheby's and
Hattula Moholy-Nagy.

Stieglitz said of his photograph, "In the early months of 1903 I stood spellbound, during a great snow storm, before the Flat Iron Building. It had just been erected on 23rd Street at the junction of Fifth Avenue and Broadway. . . . It appeared to be moving toward me like the bow of a monster ocean steamer—a picture of new America still in the making. While snow lay on the Square, I made snapshots of the building in various lights." When his father asked him why he bothered to photograph such an ugly building, Stieglitz replied, "The Flat Iron is to the United States what the Parthenon was to Greece."

Stieglitz published his image as a small photogravure in the October 1903 issue of *Camera Work*. To emphasize the height and verticality of the building, he cropped his negative on both sides and on top, making the image almost twice as high as it is wide and making what appears to be the highest point of the building almost touch the top edge of the picture. The crotch of the tree in the foreground clearly alludes to the triangular shape of the building.

As a close associate of Stieglitz's, Steichen certainly knew his photograph of the

Flatiron Building. In contrast to Stieglitz—who made most of his great early photographs of New York during wintertime, using the effects of snow to create pale, poetic images—Steichen chose a rainy day and stood on the sidewalk along the Fifth Avenue side of Madison Square, where the horse-drawn cabs waited for passengers. Although his slow film demanded daylight exposure, Steichen printed his negative to create an effect of twilight. In contrast to Stieglitz's photograph, in which no other buildings are visible and the Flatiron stands out against the natural forms of the trees, Steichen's image shows the building in its urban context—in which the filigree forms of trees still play an important role. To emphasize the Flatiron's height within his almost square format, Steichen cropped off the top of the building's prow. Steichen, who was a painter as well as a photographer, overprinted a gelatin silver print with the gum-bichromate process, which imitates painting with greater success than does any other process—and he made his print as large as a small painting. The whole image is tinted a crepuscular blue-green by the pigment in the gum emulsion. *(See notes on gum-bichromate prints and photogravures.)*

Edward Steichen,
The Flatiron, 1909
print from 1904 negative.
Greenish-blue gum bichromate over gelatin
silver print. 18¹³/₁₆ x 15¹/₈.
MMA, Stieglitz.

Steichen's romantic, twilit, painterly photograph of the Brooklyn Bridge is in strik-ing contrast to the images of the bridge that proliferated during the 1910s and 1920s, when it served as a symbol of dynamic, technological modernism. In 1902, after having lived in Paris for several years, Steichen moved to New York and began to photograph the city through soft-focus lenses, as if he were trying to impose the softness of Paris onto New York.

Evans probably did not know Steichen's photograph in 1929, though he would have seen many of Steichen's photographs in *Camera Work* when he looked through the New York Public Library's complete set of the magazine in the late 1920s. *Brooklyn Bridge,* however, was never published in *Camera Work.* Nor was it reproduced in *Steichen the Photographer* by Carl Sandburg, who was Steichen's brother-in-law. Evans reviewed that book, which appeared in 1929, in the October–December 1931 issue of *Hound and Horn,* the Harvard literary magazine founded and edited by his friend Lincoln Kirstein. Evans said there that Steichen's work was "photography off its track," and he spoke of its "technical impressiveness and spir-

itual nonexistence." Evans had more likely been influenced by some of Joseph Stella's modernistic paintings or John Marin's watercolors of the bridge than by Steichen's photograph.

In 1929 Evans lived in Brooklyn Heights near his friend Hart Crane, who was then finishing his great poem *The Bridge*, a heroic celebration of the Brooklyn Bridge as the embodiment of twentieth-century America. Three photographs from Evans's extensive bridge series were used to illustrate the edition of *The Bridge* published by the Black Sun Press in Paris in 1930—instead of the reproduction of one of Joseph Stella's paintings that the publisher had originally planned to use.

The Evans reproduced here, which is a variant of one of the photographs in *The Bridge*, must have been shot from close to where Steichen had stood. But Evans's photograph, which would have looked right at home among the sharply focused and boldly angled images of industrial forms in the 1929 *Film und Foto* exhibition in Stuttgart, is as clear, as photographic, and as modernistic as Steichen's is soft, painterly, and nostalgic.

Walker Evans,
Brooklyn Bridge, 1929.
Gelatin silver print.
$2^{1}/_{4}$ x $4^{1}/_{4}$.
Courtesy Lunn Gallery and the Estate of Walker Evans.

Frederick H. Evans,
House of Jeanne d'Arc,
Rouen, 1907.
Platinum print. 9¼ x 7⅝.
IMP/GEH. Courtesy
Evan Evans.

Evan Evans, Frederick's son, has written, "My father's photograph entitled 'House of Jeanne d'Arc, Rouen' is a most interesting one because my father told me that when he wanted to take it there was always some traffic or person in the way; so he set his 8 x 10 camera on a tripod and, whenever the road was fairly clear, took a short exposure. He did this repeatedly until he had built up the necessary time. The plate had a very slow emulsion on purpose. If you examine the print, you will see that the edge of the sunlight is blurred, as it would be during an exposure of about five minutes [since the position of the sun would have changed, even over such a short time]. He told me that people and traffic did occasionally pass, but their presence did not register owing to the shortness of the exposures."

Evans and Atget, apparently entirely through coincidence, both photographed Joan of Arc's house in 1907, and both photographed it from approximately the same spot and with similar cameras—but they made very different photographs. The

Atget shows the house much as it must have been in the fifteenth century, even though Atget usually showed no reluctance to include evidence of modernity when he photographed old buildings. Evans, on the other hand, was usually a stickler for authenticity. Before he would photograph in Ely Cathedral, for instance, he insisted on having some ugly Victorian gas fixtures removed. We can only wonder, then, why Evans didn't have the posters removed from the wall of the house. He also included a pattern of wires against the sky, which Atget eliminated by overexposing his sky. The Atget shows a heraldic sign hanging from a bracket attached to the side of the house, but the Evans does not—suggesting that the Evans was made earlier.

Atget shows the saint's house rising from dark shadow to ethereal light, perhaps alluding to Joan's fiery martyrdom, while Evans depicts the house as if it were a good person standing fast against an advancing army of shadows. (*See notes on platinum prints and albumen prints.*)

Eugène Atget,
Rue St. Romain,
Rouen, 1907.
Albumen print. 8 3/4 x 7.
MoMA, Abbott-Levy.

In 1794, soon after the French poet and revolutionary André Chénier had shifted from extreme radicalism to a more moderate position, Robespierre had him arrested and guillotined—thereby making Chénier one of the most celebrated martyrs of the Terror. He became such a popular hero that in 1896 the Italian composer Umberto Giordano wrote an opera based on his life. Eleven years later, Atget photographed the house in which Chénier was living at the time of his arrest.

By 1907 Atget had established himself as a supplier of documentary photographs to Parisian libraries and museums, to artists, and to publishers of books and postcards. Since Atget photographed the houses of Joan of Arc and André Chénier in the same year, and since Atget usually worked in series, we may surmise that he planned a series on the houses of French heroes—a project that he probably felt would have good commercial possibilities. Rather atypically, Atget photographed Chénier's house while several people were standing in front of it, but perhaps he was willing to put up with the people in order to portray the house in all its midday diversity—from the newspaper stand in front of the wine shop on the ground floor to

the birdcages in the open window on the top floor. The sign beside the second-floor window shows a waiter with a napkin draped over his arm, advertising a restaurant called La Française.

André Kertész,
Paris, 1928.
Gelatin silver print.
9$^{1}/_{2}$ x 7$^{1}/_{2}$.
© André Kertész.

When Kertész—whose friend Man Ray had shown him some of Atget's work—photographed Chénier's house in 1928, he was probably not interested at all in the history of the building. What concerned him was the black cat crossing the street. Atget, with his cumbersome view camera and slow photographic plates, had made an image of a place; but Kertész, with his newly acquired, easily handled 35mm Leica and fast film, made an image of a moment.

During his first years in Paris, Kertész became intrigued by the city's cats and often photographed them—sunning themselves in windows, wandering the streets, and being fed by an old woman. But none of his other photographs of cats has quite the ominous quality of the image reproduced here, in which the people with their backs to the viewer do not realize that they have just missed having a black cat cross their paths.

Edward Steichen,
*Heavy Roses, Voulangis,
France,* 1914.
Gelatin silver print.
16$\frac{1}{2}$ x 9$\frac{15}{16}$.
MoMA, gift of the photographer. Courtesy Joanna
T. Steichen.

Steichen was such a passionate gardener that in 1936 he persuaded the Museum of Modern Art to exhibit—as a form of modern art—the hybrid delphiniums that he had begun to develop in 1910 in his garden at Voulangis, during the second of his three long sojourns in France. That expatriate period was brought to an abrupt end in August 1914, when Germany invaded France. Steichen photographed these moribund roses on the eve of his departure for New York, and he almost certainly intended his image to be highly symbolic of the end of a great flowering of European culture.

Back in New York, Steichen continued to make close-up studies of flowers—the most spectacular of which is his 1915 shot of a lotus blossom. After the war, when he was once again living in France, he made boldly graphic extreme close-ups of flowers that have much in common with the contemporary work of German photographers Albert Renger-Patzsch and Karl Blossfeldt.

Atget, who probably never saw Steichen's image, began his extensive series of

botanical photographs with the intention of selling them to designers of textiles and wallpapers. The fairly regular spacing of the roses in the photograph reproduced here suggests that even in the 1920s, when large sales to Parisian museums freed him somewhat from financial worries, Atget continued to photograph flowers with an eye for pattern.

Unlike Steichen, who photographed a bouquet of picked roses against a black background, Atget photographed his roses in the context of a garden. Steichen's image of drooping, overripe roses is full of bittersweet pessimism, while Atget's photograph of climbing roses, open to their fullest and thriving on the vine, reflects mature optimism. Around 1920 Atget had, indeed, entered his greatest creative period. As for Steichen, the war marked the boundary between the soft-focus, "artistic" work of his youth and the sharp-focus, "commercial" work of his maturity. Perhaps Steichen sensed as he photographed the heavy roses that his youth was over.

Eugène Atget,
Roses, 1922–23.
Albumen print. $8^5/_8$ x $7^1/_8$.
MoMA, Abbott-Levy.

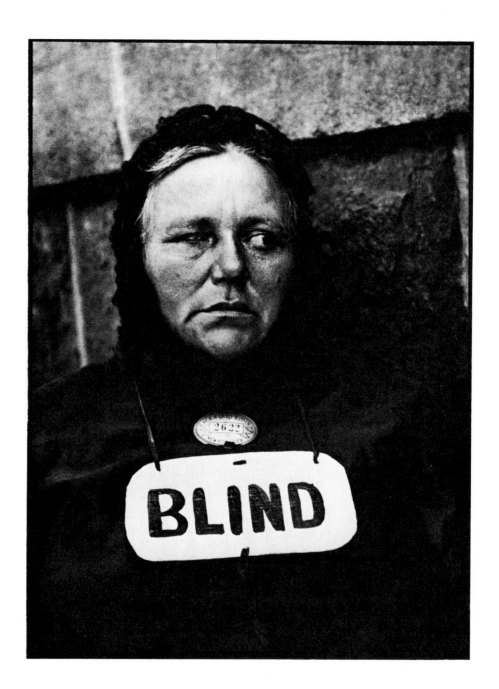

Paul Strand,
Blind Woman, New York, 1916.
Photogravure from *Camera Work.* 8¹³/₁₆ x 6⁹/₁₆.
Courtesy Lunn Gallery.

Strand made his extraordinarily powerful photograph of a blind newspaper dealer at the corner of Lexington Avenue and Thirty-fourth Street in New York with a medium format (three-and-a-quarter-by-four-and-a-quarter-inch negative) plate camera on whose side he had attached a false lens. By concealing the real lens with his sleeve, Strand could fool his subjects into thinking that he was shooting something at right angles to them. The blind woman, of course, could not have seen Strand even if he had confronted her directly with his camera, but he feared that passersby would object if they realized what he was doing.

Alfred Stieglitz was so bowled over by Strand's photographs of 1915 and 1916 that in 1917 he devoted the entire final issue of his magazine, *Camera Work,* to them. Strand's candid street portraits (which were to some extent inspired by the work of his teacher Lewis Hine) and his semi-abstractions (which were inspired by the modern painting that he saw at the famous Armory Show in New York in 1913) reached a small but influential audience. Within a few years, reverberations from Strand's work could be felt in photography all over Europe and the United States.

Model, who had intended to be a concert singer, took up photography out of financial necessity only a few months before she made her photograph of a Parisian blind man. It is highly unlikely that she would have come across Strand's photograph and been influenced by it.

Even knowing about Strand's ninety-degree trick lens, one may wonder how the photographer dared to get so close to his subject. The woman looks really formidable, and despite the blunt announcement of her crudely lettered sign, she appears to be looking at something off to the side with great suspicion and disapproval. Model's blind man looks equally sour and impatient—with the same broad, downturned mouth that Strand's woman has and a similarly illusory expression in one eye—but he is far enough away to seem much less intimidating. Indeed, he looks tiny compared to Strand's woman, who seems massive because her head and shoulders alone practically fill the entire image. Moreover, the man's sign states that he could identify the value and nationality of any coin simply by feeling it. Strand's woman looks far too proud for such tricks. *(See note on photogravures.)*

Lisette Model,
Blind Man, Paris, 1937.
Gelatin silver print.
$19^1/_2$ x $15^5/_8$.
© Lisette Model.
Courtesy Sander Gallery.

Eugène Atget,
Circus Sideshow Painting,
c. 1920.
Albumen print. 6³/₄ x 8¹/₂.
Private collection.

Atget's photograph of a sideshow painting again demonstrates his love of circuses *(see his* Fôire du Trône, *page 47).* As in his other photographs of vernacular artwork decorating circus structures, one may detect a mixture of genuine, almost childlike delight in the spirit of the circus and a sardonic sense of the naïve artifice on which the circus depends for its magic. Although the painting of the fire in the jungle is a wonderful example of circus art in its own right, worthy of being photographed for posterity, Atget has deliberately included enough of the canvas tent above and the exposed beams below to undermine the painting's immediacy. These painted panels, somewhat battered from having been put up and taken down many times, may have held a special poignance for Atget, who had for many years traveled through the French provinces with a theatrical repertoire company. Indeed, the space in the photograph looks somewhat like a stage, and one can only wonder whether the dramatic painting of panic-stricken animals (incongruously including an American porcupine and an Australian kangaroo) was a backdrop for an act, an advertisement, or an attraction in its own right.

In the early 1930s, when Shahn and Walker Evans shared a studio in Greenwich Village, Evans introduced Shahn to Atget's photographs. Although Atget's photograph of the circus painting is not reproduced in the 1930 book *Atget, Photographe de Paris*, which was then the only publication on Atget, several photographs of circus sideshow facades and numerous images showing naïvely painted signs were illustrated.

Shahn's photographs of the 1930s may be roughly divided into two categories—warm, sensitive, and sympathetic pictures of people and witty, sometimes even surreal images of signs. In this latter category he was greatly influenced by Atget and Evans. Like the painting in Atget's photograph, the poster in Shahn's is punctuated by vertical lines that suggest the bars of a cage. It also juxtaposes incongruous animals, including a polar bear and a tiger. But the Atget suggests the presence of the circus, while the Shahn suggests its passing. The poster that Shahn photographed was already peeling, and life had presumably returned to normal after the brief excitement of the circus.

Ben Shahn,
Circus Poster, Smithland, Kentucky, 1935.
Gelatin silver print.
6^1/$_2$ x 9^9/$_{16}$.
LC.

Kertész's Hungarian photographs from the 1910s fall into several categories—soft-focus, painterly genre subjects; straightforward reportage of military and rural life; tender and sentimental (though never maudlin) images of women, children, and lovers; and early experiments with photographic distortion. The affectionate but witty, forthrightly composed, medium-sharply focused photograph of a scene from everyday life that is reproduced here contains elements of the first three categories and looks ahead to the work that Kertész would do in Paris and New York over the course of the following sixty years.

It is quite possible that this photograph was among the thirty-five prints that Kertész showed in the exhibition of modern European photography that Julien Levy mounted in his New York gallery in 1932. If so, Shahn probably would have seen it. The following year Shahn definitely saw at Levy's gallery Henri Cartier-Bresson's 1932 photograph of a man in Brussels peering through the loosely woven canvas of a circus tent. Shahn frequently cited Cartier-Bresson as an important influence on his own photographic work. Like Cartier-Bresson, Shahn used a 35mm

camera, but unlike the French photographer, Shahn equipped his camera with an angle viewfinder whose prism allowed him to face ninety degrees away from his subject *(see Strand,* Blind Woman, *page 80).*

In contrast to Kertész, Shahn never thought of himself primarily as a photographer. For Shahn, photography was a way of making notes for his paintings. He zeroed in on what interested him and didn't worry too much about whether anything else in the picture was cut off by the picture edge. When he made his photograph of men looking through a fence, he was mainly concerned with the men at the sides of the picture, and when, in 1938, he based a painting on this photograph, he simply eliminated the middle man and put a poster in the empty space.

Although the cutoff figures in Shahn's photographs may initially have arisen out of expediency, he used his technique to make some of the strongest and most memorable photographs in the Resettlement Administration's files. Particularly in the photographs of the Southeast that he made in 1935, Shahn's cutoff figures eloquently convey a sense of the chaos of the time.

Ben Shahn,
*Sunday Football Game,
Scott's Run, West Virginia,*
1935.
Gelatin silver print.
$7^{3}/_{16}$ x $8^{7}/_{8}$.
Fogg. Courtesy Mrs.
Bernarda Shahn.

Edward Weston, *Nude*, 1920. Platinum print. 8¹³/₁₆ x 7½. MoMA. Courtesy Cole Weston.

In 1920 Weston, who until then had been a commercial portrait photographer, became serious about photography as as art form and began his life's work. Like many photographers of the time, he believed that photography could be an art only if it imitated painting. He therefore used a special soft-focus lens to give his nudes and portraits a diffuse, ethereal quality—an effect whose subtleties of tone he developed further by printing on platinum paper.

This nude torso is one of the most sensuous and luminous of Weston's early works. It also clearly prefigures his later interest in using the nude to make photographs that approach abstraction. Weston himself was proud of this image, and it is one of the few soft-focus photographs whose negative he did not destroy after he had become committed to the pursuit of the greatest possible clarity in his work.

Man Ray, who almost certainly had no opportunity to see Weston's photograph, wrote in his autobiography that one of his first experiments with movies, in 1923, included a shot of "a nude torso moving in front of a striped curtain with the

sunlight coming through." The photograph reproduced here is clearly related to that film image. The original conception could well have derived from the title of his 1916 abstract painting *The Rope Dancer Accompanies Herself with Shadows.*

In the early 1920s, Man Ray was preoccupied with shadows. His most important photographic works of that time were his Rayographs, which were made by placing small objects directly on sheets of photographic paper and then exposing them to light so that their shadows would create bizarre and virtually abstract images. Even his conventional photographs of the period focus on the weird shadows of such objects as an eggbeater and a floodlight.

It is appropriate that the pattern on Weston's nude is one of light, while that on Man Ray's is one of shadow. Throughout his career Weston, who was essentially a classicist, was concerned with the nude body and the revelatory powers of light, while Man Ray, a radical modernist, was fascinated by the enchanting powers of darkness and shadow. *(See note on platinum prints.)*

Man Ray,
Torso, 1923.
Gelatin silver print.
$7^1/_8$ x $5^5/_8$.
MoMA, gift of James Thrall Soby. Courtesy Mrs. Juliet Man Ray.

Cunningham did relatively little photography in the late teens and the early twenties, since she had her hands full with her three young sons—the first born in 1915, followed by twins in 1917. In 1920, when her husband, Roi Partridge, began teaching art at Mills College, the family moved from San Francisco to Oakland. In contrast to this striking, sharply focused semi-abstraction of the stone steps in the Mills College amphitheater, most of Cunningham's few photographs from this period are romantic, soft-focus portraits and nudes.

Cunningham and Edward Weston, who met in 1923, had a running controversy over who influenced whom. Weston had begun his transition from soft to sharp focus in 1922, but he didn't become firmly committed to a style of maximum clarity until about 1924. Cunningham claimed that this transition was reinforced by his having seen her work in 1923, but her own photographs didn't become as consistently sharply focused and design-oriented as Weston's until about 1929, by which time she had seen much of Weston's work.

Cunningham probably met Modotti through Weston in 1923. Late that year

Modotti moved with Weston to Mexico, where she herself became an excellent photographer. She remained in Mexico after Weston returned to California in 1926, but she and Weston continued to exchange work by mail. It is entirely possible that Cunningham had seen Modotti's photograph of the stadium before she made her own, since the visual evidence suggests that Cunningham, who was often unclear about the dating of her work, didn't actually make her photograph of the amphitheater until the late twenties.

The primary effect of the Modotti is that the eye is grabbed by the strong receding lines and pulled to the upper left corner, where the lines converge. Because Modotti clearly set up her tripod on the center step and aimed straight ahead, the viewer has a sense of being able to penetrate into the picture. Cunningham's higher viewpoint, looking down on the steps, makes her photograph more removed from the subject and thus more abstract. In addition to the sensuousness of the overall curving configuration, Cunningham may have delighted in the way the shadows on the risers of the steps flatten out and become abstract black shapes.

Tina Modotti,
Stadium, Mexico City, 1926.
Gelatin silver print.
7⁹/₁₆ x 9⁷/₁₆.
MoMA.

Lewis W. Hine,
Powerhouse Mechanic,
c. 1921.
Gelatin silver print.
9⅝ x 7.
IMP/GEH.

After fifteen years of documenting the plight of immigrants and the horrors of child labor, Hine unexpectedly turned his camera, around 1920, to celebrating the machine as the liberator of modern society. When, in 1921, he published his photograph of a powerhouse mechanic in *The Survey,* an important magazine dealing with social and labor problems, the caption optimistically stated, "Machinists, electricians, toolmakers, engineers are of the ancient line of grooms, and hostlers, and veterinaries. Why not, for they are the trainers of ten thousand horse-power." Although Hine evinced an attitude that Charlie Chaplin effectively ridiculed in his 1936 film *Modern Times,* his photograph of the warmly human mechanic—who has, however, posed as stiffly as if he were trying to imitate a machine—is a haunting image of the tensions between man and machine.

Hine's photograph has an antecedent in a 1908 image by the English Pictorialist photographer Malcolm Arbuthnot, in which a laborer is bent over in front of a huge cartwheel as he digs with a pitchfork. Hine could have seen Arbuthnot's photograph through Alfred Stieglitz, who knew both men, or in the 1908 edition of the influen-

tial annual *Photograms of the Year,* which published a line drawing of the image. Hine used an updated version of his own photograph—showing an older mechanic and a more modern turbine—on the half-title page of his 1932 book *Men at Work.*

Bourke-White, who was intensely interested in machinery and labor, must have seen Hine's photographs in *The Survey* during the 1920s. In 1930, soon after she had begun to work for the newly founded *Fortune* magazine, Bourke-White persuaded the Soviet authorities to let her photograph Russian industry—and that at a time when no Western photographers were allowed into the country. She later wrote, "With my enthusiasm for the machine as an object of beauty, I felt the story of a nation trying to industrialize almost overnight was just cut out for me."

Although she complained that the workmen at Dnieperstroi were "like children playing with new toys," her photograph of a man tightening a bolt on a generator shell gives no hint of frivolousness. On the contrary, one senses the seriousness and concentration of the man and the dangers of his job—emphasized by Bourke-White's vertiginous camera angle.

Margaret Bourke-White,
A Generator Shell,
Dnieperstroi, 1930.
Gelatin silver print.
$9^{11}/_{16}$ x $6^{5}/_{8}$.
Courtesy Life.

Ralph Steiner,
Typewriter Keys, 1921.
Gelatin silver print. 8 x 6.
Courtesy Sotheby's
and the artist.

Ralph Steiner made this photograph of typewriter keys as a design exercise at the Clarence White School of Photography in New York. Around the turn of the century, White had been a member of Alfred Stieglitz's inner circle of Pictorialists. But when Stieglitz, in the early teens, became an apostate to the cause of painterly photography, White broke with him and founded his school, where he continued to advocate an aesthetic based on Japanese prints and Whistler's paintings.

Although Steiner didn't like the rigid, formulistic approach to design that prevailed at White's school, he managed to make there this study of a typewriter, which is as modern and as photographic as anything that was being done about that time at the Bauhaus *(see Moholy-Nagy, page 51).* Indeed, Steiner's photograph has much in common with German photographs of the 1920s, particularly those of Albert Renger-Patzsch, the leader of the New Objectivists, who were reacting against the extreme subjectivism of the Pictorialists. Like many of Renger-Patzsch's photographs, Steiner's typewriter study is a close-up detail of a functionally designed

utilitarian object isolated from its surroundings. Even the repetitious, all-over pattern of the keys echoes Renger-Patzsch's frequently used device of photographing numerous examples of a manufactured object together.

Although Modotti made a rather similar close-up of a typewriter, she certainly did not conceive of her photograph as a mere exercise in design. By 1929 she had become an ardent member of the Mexican Communist party, and photography had become for her a means of making revolutionary social statements—the visual counterpart of the verbal statement that her friend Mella, a young Cuban revolutionary, was writing on his typewriter. In Modotti's eyes, the typewriter was a tool of the revolution, worthy of being photographed not on account of its intrinsic beauty but on account of what could be accomplished with it.

Modotti's photograph of Mella's typewriter takes on an added dimension when we learn that later in 1929 Modotti was accused of having murdered Mella. Nothing, however, could be proved against her.

Tina Modotti,
*The Typewriter of Julio
Antonio Mella
(Number 22),* 1929.
Gelatin silver print.
$9^{3}/_{8}$ x $7^{1}/_{2}$.
MoMA.

Both of these images were made when the photographers were very young—before they had begun their professional careers. Steiner has written of the body of work to which this bicyclist-and-shadow image belongs: "These early photographs were made with a 4 x 5 Korona View camera and a rapid rectilinear lens—often on glass plates, because an old photographer had told me that you could never get the quality on film that glass plates assured." He also said that what saved him from falling into either the pretentiousness of Pictorialism or the sterility of design-oriented photography was his sense of humor. Although this shot of a bicyclist may at first seem more elegant than humorous, there is a fine touch of wit in the seeming interchangeability of the bicyclist and his shadow—and, indeed, if you turn the picture upside down, the shadow seems to become the bicyclist and vice versa. This effect could only have been obtained by silhouetting the bicyclist in bright midday sunlight and shooting from a distance in order to obliterate all his features.

The device of photographing people and their shadows was so prevalent during the 1920s that it eventually became something of a cliché, but Steiner's photograph

Alfred Eisenstaedt,
*Bicyclist, Holsteiner Ufer,
Berlin,* 1928.
Gelatin silver print.
$9^7/_{16}$ x $7^9/_{16}$.
Courtesy the artist.

was one of the first of the genre. There was no way that Eisenstaedt could have seen Steiner's photograph before he made his own. Steiner did, however, show ten photographs in the Deutsche Werkbund exhibition *Film und Foto* in Stuttgart in 1929, and it is possible that the bicyclist-and-shadow picture was among them. This is particularly intriguing in view of the fact that Moholy-Nagy, one of the organizers of the exhibition, made a similarly composed bicyclist-and-shadow picture of his own around 1930—though he dispensed with the mirror-image effect.

There is no confusing the bicyclist and his shadow in Eisenstaedt's photograph, for he made his image in raking early morning or late afternoon light that elongated the shadow and cast a light soft enough that it allowed the bicyclist's clothing to remain distinct. Like Steiner, Eisenstaedt used glass dry plates, but the latter's measured only one and three-quarters by two and three-eighths inches, the size used by the Ermanox camera that was popular among photojournalists until the 35mm Leica was accepted as the standard tool of the trade. Although the Ermanox was small, it was usually tripod-mounted—as Steiner's heavy camera had to be.

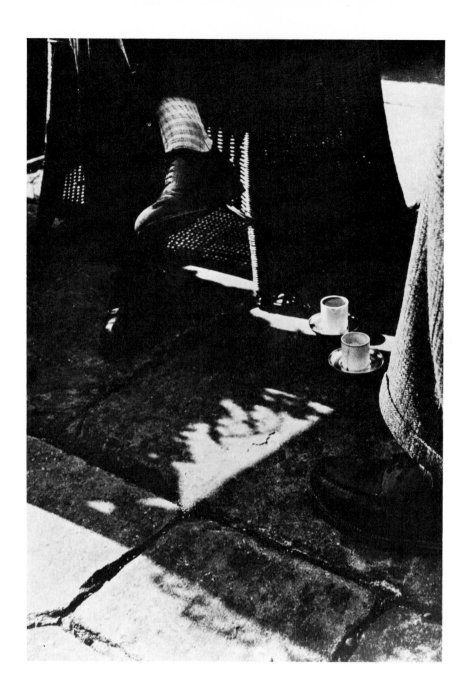

László Moholy-Nagy,
The Cup of Coffee, c. 1925.
Gelatin silver print.
11¼ x 8⅜.
Larson Coll. © William
Larson. Courtesy Hattula
Moholy-Nagy.

Perhaps because Moholy-Nagy made many of his most interesting photographs while he was on vacation from the Bauhaus, the images tend to reflect a certain playfulness, a certain delight in breaking the rules of photographic composition. *The Cup of Coffee* almost looks like the kind of picture that one might make while, without even looking through the viewfinder, one shoots off the first few frames of a new roll of film in order to get to the first frame that is safe to use. And yet the image is both situationally intriguing and aesthetically satisfying. The composition—filled with diagonals, isolated forms, and extreme contrasts of light and dark—is reminiscent of Moholy-Nagy's abstract photograms of the period, but *The Cup of Coffee* is not an abstract photograph. It provides just enough information about the two men and their situation so that one can hardly help trying to imagine the scene beyond the edges of the image. Moholy-Nagy, however, would not have approved of this approach, since he felt that the camera's ability to focus on purely visual phenomena and to record them without any peripheral distractions pointed the way to objective, nonassociational, unsentimental seeing. He was, after all, working at a

time when the avant-garde believed that science and technology could create a utopian civilization.

By the time Model made her photograph of a gambler, dreams of utopia had given way to the nightmarish prospect of war. When Model went to visit her mother in Nice in 1937, she made an extensive series of photographs of the wealthy men and women who whiled away their afternoons sitting in the wicker chairs along the city's Promenade des Anglais. To make most of the photographs, Model, who probably could not have seen Moholy-Nagy's picture, got very close to her subjects and crouched very low. As a result, her subjects—who range from the spoiled and haughty to the sinister and cruel—loom menacingly over the viewer. The series is such a powerful indictment of the French upper class that when Ralph Steiner, who was then picture editor of the newspaper *PM*, published several of the photographs in 1941, he ran them under the title "Why France Fell."

It is easy to see how this photograph of a gambler might have influenced Model's student Diane Arbus, who also had a penchant for photographing the sinister.

Lisette Model,
Gambler, French Riviera, 1938.
Gelatin silver print.
$13^7/_8$ x $10^1/_4$.
Courtesy Sander Gallery.
© Lisette Model.

László Moholy-Nagy,
The Diving Board, c. 1925.
Gelatin silver print.
11⅛ x 8⅛.
MoMA. Courtesy Hattula
Moholy-Nagy.

In Moholy-Nagy's *Diving Board* one can again see, as in *The Cup of Coffee (see page 96),* the random-seeming, fragmented, diagonal composition that the photographer favored. Moreover, the composition is strikingly reminiscent of some of Kazimir Malevich's abstract paintings of the 1910s. Malevich, a leader of the Russian avant-garde who believed that abstract art was a spiritual manifestation of the new social and political order, often painted rectangles arranged diagonally on white backgrounds, as if they were floating in space. Moholy-Nagy was familiar with Malevich's work through the Bauhaus, with which the Russian painter had frequent contact. By applying Malevich's style of composition to banal subject matter, Moholy-Nagy irreverently brought the Russian's high-flown spiritualism down to earth. And yet, at the same time, Moholy-Nagy might have thought that he was

vindicating Malevich by discovering his highly subjective configurations in the objective world.

Erwitt has always been even more playful than Moholy-Nagy ever was. His photograph of sunbathers in Brighton, however, does not seem at all funny. It seems, on the contrary, disturbingly ominous. And yet when one looks at it in the context of Erwitt's other work, one may suspect that the joke is that the person who seems to be approaching the sunbathers with malicious intent was actually a perfectly innocent passerby. Erwitt delights in demonstrating how easily the camera can be made to lie.

Moholy-Nagy believed that the camera was an objective recorder of purely optical facts. Erwitt understands that the camera can be an outrageously subjective fabricator of fictions.

Elliott Erwitt,
Brighton, England, 1970.
Gelatin silver print.
$6^5/_{16}$ x $9^1/_2$.
Courtesy Magnum.

In 1923, when Steichen returned to the United States after a long stay in Europe, he
became chief photographer for Condé Nast Publications and rented a studio in the
Bryant Park Studios building on the corner of Sixth Avenue (now the Avenue of the
Americas) and Fortieth Street. He shot this view of West Fortieth Street, looking
toward Broadway, from one of the windows of his studio.

Sheeler's photograph is usually assumed to belong to the series of rather cubistic
New York views that he began soon after moving from Philadelphia to New York in
1919. Most of those photographs, however, look down from the tops of skyscrapers
onto configurations of lower buildings, while this view was shot with the camera
pointing straight ahead. If this photograph had really been made around 1920, then
it would have been safe to deduce that Steichen had seen it, since he was a friend of
Sheeler's and employed him to do fashion and portrait work for Condé Nast from
1923 to 1929. But since the Sheeler shows (in the middle distance on the right) a

massive office building that was built in 1924–25, while the Steichen, which is usually dated 1925, shows a row of small buildings on that spot, it is evident that
Steichen made his photograph before Sheeler made his.

Steichen and Sheeler framed their views so differently that it is not immediately
apparent that the buildings in the foregrounds of both photographs are the same.
Furthermore, Sheeler, who prided himself on his detached objectivity, made a photograph that is a meticulously composed and semi-abstract pattern of cool grays.
Steichen's photograph, taken at night by moonlight—supplemented by electric light
in the street—is a highly romantic image.

Fortieth Street has changed remarkably little since 1925. The building on the left
in both photographs (110 West Fortieth Street) is still there, though the view of it
from the Bryant Park Studios is largely obstructed by a modern building. The
building on the right has been replaced, but the others are intact.

Charles Sheeler,
West Fortieth Street,
New York, c. 1926.
Gelatin silver print.
$6^3/_4$ x $4^1/_2$.
Courtesy Zabriskie Gallery
and Lane Foundation.

Cunningham made her series of close-up photographs of flowers in the middle and late 1920s, when caring for her three small sons prevented her from going out on portrait assignments. The magnolia, one of the first in the series, is halfway between her early romantic, soft-focus nudes and the sharp-focus, structure- and design-oriented close-ups of flowers that Karl Blossfeldt and Albert Renger-Patzsch (who were unknown to Cunningham) were then making in Germany. The sensuousness and luminosity of the magnolia's petals, which suggest the soft skin and supple forms of a nude, are closer to the qualities of the flower studies that Georgia O'Keeffe was then beginning to paint than to anything in photography.

Edward Weston, who with Steichen organized the American section of the landmark *Film und Foto* exhibition in Stuttgart in 1929, chose several of Cunningham's flower studies, including the magnolia, for the exhibition. Man Ray, who also ex-

hibited, certainly saw the show when a large portion of it traveled to Paris in 1930. His magnolia belongs to a series of flower studies he made in 1931 (not 1925, as sometimes stated), clearly stimulated by work—including Cunningham's—that he saw in *Film und Foto*.

In contrast to Cunningham's photograph, in which there is no readable background except for a glimpse of a leaf in the upper right corner, Man Ray's image distinctly shows the picked flower in a black-and-white checked basket. Both photographs mix the beauty of the flower with a slightly sinister quality. Cunningham's image, which she initially entitled *The Tower of Jewels*, vaguely suggests a many-armed Hindu god protected by hooded cobras, while the photograph by Man Ray, who was interested in the works of the Marquis de Sade, depicts beauty that has been plucked and trapped and is already beginning to wither.

Man Ray,
Magnolia, 1931.
Gelatin silver print.
$10^3/_4$ x $8^7/_8$.
MoMA, gift of James Thrall
Soby. Courtesy Mrs. Juliet
Man Ray.

Edward Weston,
Ship's Bow, Alameda,
San Francisco, 1925.
Gelatin silver print. 7½ x 9½.
AIC. Courtesy Cole Weston.

Although Weston had experimented with sharp-focus photography in 1922, it was only in Mexico in 1924 that he finally discarded his soft-focus lens and became obsessed with maximum clarity. He made this photograph of a ship's bow in 1925, during a six-month visit to California before returning to Mexico for another year.

Like most of Weston's photographs, that of the ship's bow was made with an eight- by ten-inch view camera and natural light. To avoid the distortion and loss of detail that often occurs in enlargements, Weston usually made his prints the same size as his negatives—using the entire image precisely as he had composed it on the ground-glass screen of his camera. He felt that cropping an image was tantamount to admitting one's failure to see photographically. Although in 1925 he was still making platinum prints, by 1930 he had switched to high-gloss silver papers, which offered much greater contrasts and more details in dark areas. The print reproduced here is a silver print made by Weston's son Brett under his father's supervision in the 1950s, when Weston himself was too ill to do his own printing.

Although Weston exhibited a photograph of a ship's bow (either this one or another from the series) at the great *Film und Foto* exhibition in Stuttgart in 1929,

this photograph does not seem to have been published anywhere that Evans might have seen it. Evans made his photograph in the spring of 1931, at which time he and his friend Lincoln Kirstein were driving around New England in search of nineteenth-century houses for Evans to photograph. Like Weston, Evans used a tripod-mounted view camera and contact printed his negative.

Weston's photograph is filled with the sort of crisp lines and bold contrasts that he had begun to seek in reaction against his soft-focus style. The image is, in many respects, halfway between his truncated nude of 1920 *(see page 86)* and his almost surreal 1939 photograph of rubber dummies *(see page 156),* of which the figurehead offers a foreshadowing. When Evans made his photograph, in which there are no references to the twentieth century—such as the telephone poles and wires in Weston's photograph—he was surely thinking of the *Pequod,* which sailed from New Bedford in search of Moby Dick. Oddly, Evans's emphasis on pure form is in the spirit of Weston's classic work of the 1920s, while the Weston, which shows the ship's prow in context, seems close to Evans's characteristic juxtaposition of elements from the nineteenth and twentieth centuries.

Walker Evans,
New Bedford, Massachusetts,
1931.
Gelatin silver print.
6$\frac{1}{8}$ x 7$\frac{1}{4}$.
Courtesy the Estate of
Walker Evans.

Alexander Rodchenko,
Balconies, 1926.
Gelatin silver print.
16 x 10½.
Private collection.

In 1928 Rodchenko wrote, "The most interesting visual angles of our age are the bird's eye view and the worm's eye view, and we must adopt them in our work." Rodchenko's intention in making photographs from angles other than those of normal vision was "to show usual things in unusual ways." In this he followed the teachings of his friend Viktor Shklovsky, a literary critic, who claimed that "the technique of art is to make things unfamiliar and to make forms difficult, to increase the difficulty and length of perception, because the process of perception is an aesthetic end in itself and must be prolonged."

Later in 1928 the magazine *Soviet Foto* published Rodchenko's *Balconies* next to a variant of the Moholy-Nagy, along with an anonymous letter accusing Rodchenko of plagiarism. Rodchenko replied that he had published his photograph in 1926 and that the Moholy-Nagy was not published until later. He went on to say that he

esteemed Moholy-Nagy, to whom he had often sent photographs. The two men had frequent communication and learned much from each other.

Moholy-Nagy reproduced his own photograph of balconies in the second edition of his highly influential book *Painting Photography Film*, published by the Bauhaus in 1927, with the caption "The optical truth of the perspectival construction." His photograph of balconies on the newly constructed Bauhaus building in Dessau does indeed demonstrate how the lines in a picture converge to render distance.

The balconies in the Rodchenko, which almost seem to float in space, look as if they could continue in a series extending infinitely upward. The man on the top balcony of the Moholy-Nagy emphatically terminates the series in that photograph. The contact that is established between the man and the viewer makes the Moholy-Nagy seem more humanistic than the strictly formalistic Rodchenko.

László Moholy-Nagy,
Bauhaus Balconies,
Dessau, 1926.
Gelatin silver print.
19¹/₂ x 15¹/₂.
IMP/GEH. Courtesy
Hattula Moholy-Nagy.

Atget made his great series of photographs of store windows with mannequins and reflections in the year or so before his death in 1927. The older Atget got, the more obviously poetic—and the less obviously documentary—his work became. This photograph of mannequins in the window of a men's clothing store on the avenue des Gobelins in Paris, although it does document the styles and prices of 1926, primarily documents Atget's wittily literal perception of the interaction between the mannequins and the reflections. The ghostly torso and optimistically smiling face of the mannequin at the right dwarf the grandiose doorway from which they appear to be emerging; the mannequin in the middle of the window looks as if he has just picked up someone's gloves and is wondering how he can use this courtesy to his advantage; while the mannequin at the left looks intelligent and introspective. The mannequin in the right foreground has, in the best surrealist tradition, an ornamental finial instead of a head, and the hand intruding at the extreme right appears to be reaching for something on the grille covering the roots of a tree on the pavement.

The surrealistic tendencies of Atget's late work interested his neighbor Man Ray,

who published several of the photographs in the avant-garde magazine *La Révolution Surréaliste*. Atget, however, did not consider himself a Surrealist and asked Man Ray not to identify him as the photographer.

Evans probably first saw Atget's photograph of mannequins in the book *Atget, Photographe de Paris*, which he reviewed in 1931 for *Hound and Horn*. Evans, who frequently cited Atget as one of the photographers whom he admired most, wrote that Atget's "general note is lyrical understanding of the street, trained observation of it, special feeling for patina, eye for revealing detail, over all of which is thrown a poetry which is . . . the projection of Atget's own person." Although Evans, like Atget, used an eight- by ten-inch camera for much of his work, he used a 35mm camera for this obvious homage to Atget. The reflections of Evans's head, arms, and camera are just barely visible around the shoulders of the unfinished jacket, while the reflection of a curious passerby can be seen above the tailor-mannequin. The superimposition of the reflected office buildings on the rows of drawers may be a droll comment on offices in general.

Walker Evans,
Third Avenue, New York,
1959.
Gelatin silver print.
$7^{15}/_{16}$ x $5^{3}/_{8}$.
Courtesy the Estate of
Walker Evans.

Alexander Rodchenko,
Street, 1927.
Gelatin silver print.
15³/₄ x 10¹/₂.
Private collection.

By 1927 Rodchenko was in his prime as a photojournalist. He had become skilled at supplying attention-grabbing shots for magazine covers, and he had discovered how to communicate the spirit of a society turned topsy-turvy by political, economic, and industrial revolution. His photograph of pedestrians and their shadows, seen from a very high viewpoint directly over their heads, is a superb example of his style at that time; it is dramatically disorienting, concise, witty, and composed with a strong feeling for abstract design. The street, the sidewalk, and the pedestrians' radically foreshortened bodies are reduced to abstractions, and paradoxically, only the shadows have a semblance of reality.

Like Rodchenko, Umbo was a painter turned photojournalist. After studying painting and design at the Bauhaus from 1921 to 1923, he became involved in making movies. It was only in 1928 that he began to work in the newly emerging field of photojournalism. Umbo was a forerunner of the New Wave photojournalists of today—sophisticated, clever, and slick.

Since Russian photography was all the rage in Germany in the late 1920s, it is

quite likely that Umbo could have seen Rodchenko's photograph. The similarity between the images seems too great to be purely coincidental, though the idea of photographing pedestrians and their shadows from above was "in the air" in Europe in the 1920s and the early 1930s. As early as 1923, the Hungarian photographer Martin Munkacsi had made an oblique overhead shot of schoolchildren and their shadows, but it is not as extreme in its conception as Rodchenko's image. In 1931 Kertész, who was then working in Paris, also photographed schoolchildren and their shadows, but his viewpoint was much lower than Rodchenko's.

Although Umbo used the same idea, roughly the same composition, and approximately the same distance from his subject that Rodchenko had used, the German chose a sidewalk with a large hole that was only partially covered with planks. The uncovered part of the hole, whose blackness is identical to that of the shadows, has swallowed up the head of one of the pedestrians. And, in general, all of the shadows in the Umbo are harder to decipher than those in the Rodchenko. Umbo did not photograph a weird street; he made a weird photograph.

Umbo (Otto Umbehr),
Weird Street, 1928.
Gelatin silver print.
$8^5/_8$ x $6^1/_2$.
Private collection.

In 1927 Vaughan Flannery, art director of the Philadelphia advertising firm of N. W. Ayer and Son, for which Sheeler did much free-lance photography throughout the 1920s, persuaded the Ford Motor Company to commission Sheeler to make a photographic documentation of its newly expanded plant at River Rouge, Michigan, just outside Detroit. In the course of his six weeks at the plant, Sheeler made only thirty-two photographs, but they were among the finest works of his career.

In this photograph of smokestacks and crossed passageways, Sheeler was clearly influenced by the photographs of the Armco steel mill in Middleton, Ohio, that Edward Weston had made on his way to New York in 1922. While Weston was in New York, he met Sheeler and admired his photographs of the city, calling them "the finest architectural photographs I have ever seen." Sheeler returned the compliment by emulating the heroic, modernistic style of Weston's Armco photographs. Although industrial subjects were prevalent in Germany during the 1920s, they were still fairly radical for serious American photographers.

Evans probably first saw Sheeler's photograph of smokestacks and passageways

in the March 1930 issue of *Arts et Métiers Graphiques,* a special issue devoted to photography, which Evans reviewed for *Hound and Horn* in 1931, though Evans made no mention of Sheeler in his review. Four other photographs from the Ford series had been published in *Hound and Horn* in 1930.

Evans made a series of photographs of the Ford plant in 1947 for a *Fortune* photo-essay that was never published. Several of his images are strikingly similar to pictures by Sheeler, but where Sheeler had composed his photographs vertically, Evans often framed his corresponding photographs horizontally. For his photograph of smokestacks and crossed passageways, Evans set up his camera farther back and farther to the right than Sheeler had, so that he could include a passageway high in the foreground. Sheeler also used the stacks as much darker, more emphatic rhythmic accents than Evans did, but otherwise the two photographs reflect such similar sensibilities that if one saw them without any identification, one might reasonably assume that they were variant images made by the same photographer at the same time.

Walker Evans,
Ford Motor Company Plant, River Rouge, Michigan, 1947.
Gelatin silver print.
6¼ x 8.
Courtesy the Estate of Walker Evans.

André Kertész,
Meudon, 1928.
Gelatin silver print.
8 1/2 x 5 7/8.
© André Kertész.

Soon after Kertész moved to Paris in 1925, he met Man Ray, who in turn introduced him to his circle of Surrealist friends. It is, then, not at all surprising that a distinct element of Surrealism began to appear in Kertész's work in the late 1920s. *Meudon,* one of Kertész's most surrealistic photographs, looks as if it could be a still from a Surrealist film such as Luis Buñuel's *L'Age d'Or* or Jean Cocteau's *Le Sang d'un Poète,* neither of which was completed until 1930. Kertész's photograph is also strongly reminiscent of the work of the Italian metaphysical painter Giorgio de Chirico, in many of whose paintings of the 1910s arcades figure prominently.

Meudon, which Kertész shot with the 35mm Leica that he had recently bought, is an extraordinary image of a frozen moment. But the photograph does not simply record the ominous conjunction of a train speeding in one direction and a man walking in the opposite direction with a mysterious package wrapped in newspaper under his arm. It also collapses the passage of centuries into a single image. The

eighteenth-century houses, the nineteenth-century viaduct, and the twentieth-century man create a disturbing warp in the continuum of perceived time.

Brandt, who worked in Paris as Man Ray's assistant from 1929 to 1931, undoubtedly saw *Meudon* when he got to know Kertész through Man Ray. Brandt has, in any case, acknowledged Kertész's work as as important influence on his own.

Train Leaving Newcastle is a quintessential Brandt image—black with the grime and soot of coal-mining, coal-burning England. Whether or not a Brandt photograph actually depicts a coal miner with a blackened face or a factory belching smoke, it will probably cast a dark, gritty pall over its subject—an effect often enhanced by the graininess and high contrast of Brandt's prints.

Train Leaving Newcastle is so dark with the smudge of nineteenth-century technology that it could well be used to illustrate William Blake's famous line about England's "dark Satanic mills."

Bill Brandt,
Train Leaving Newcastle,
1937.
Gelatin silver print.
8⁹/₁₆ x 7⁵/₁₆.
Courtesy Lunn Gallery.
© Bill Brandt.

André Kertész,
Paris, 1929.
Gelatin silver print.
8¹/₂ x 6.
© André Kertész.

In Kertész's photograph of wooden horses and women, as in his photograph of Meudon *(see page 114),* there is a sharp edge of Surrealist irony. Indeed, mannequins, dummies, dolls, and masks that transferred human or animal features to the inanimate became favored subjects for Surrealist photographers in the late 1920s and the 1930s.

Kertész's photograph may be read as a wry comment on fairy tales in the modern world. The team of magical horses who should be pulling the "coach" have been unceremoniously stacked—some of them upside down on top of their fellows—inside the vehicle, which turns out to be a circus wagon. The four figures appear to look out of the cart with expressions of anticipation, and the one at the left looks as if she is craning her neck to see where they are. The rope against her neck introduces a note of high drama, for it suggests that these lovely ladies have been abducted, transformed into mannequins by a wicked enchanter, and forced into a life of servitude in the circus.

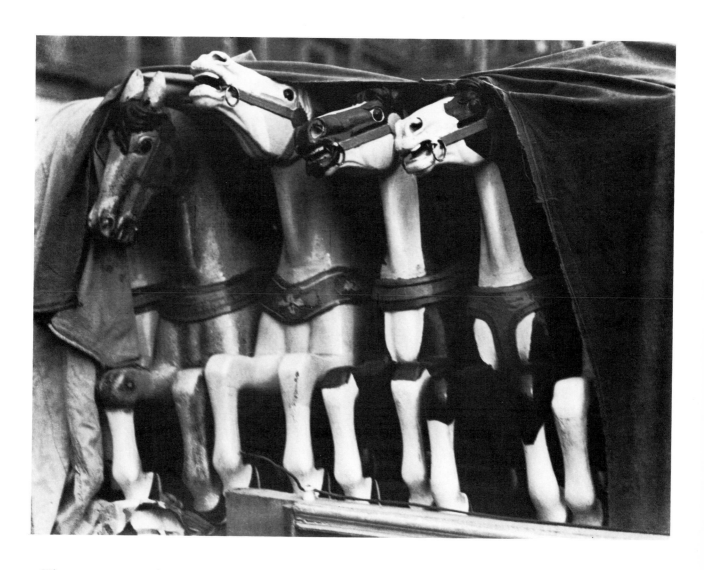

Nineteen twenty-nine was an important year for Alvarez Bravo, for, at Tina Modotti's suggestion, he sent a portfolio of his photographs—possibly including *Los Obstaculos*—to Edward Weston in California and received an encouraging response. Alvarez Bravo did not know Kertész's work at that time, and he was just beginning to become aware of the Surrealist movement that was taking over all of the arts in Europe. He was working for the most part out a sense of the surreal, the grotesque, and the ironic that is native to Mexico.

The year before Alvarez Bravo made *Los Obstaculos*, he had photographed a single wooden horse, grinning timidly through the part between a tasseled curtain and a wall. That was a mild-mannered steed, but the horses in *Los Obstaculos* are, except for the introspective-looking one at the left, reckless and frenzied. They could be the horses of the four riders of the Apocalypse. Or, more in keeping with their obvious woodenness, they could be the sort of horse that D. H. Lawrence's young hero rode to his feverish inspirations in "The Rocking-Horse Winner."

Manuel Alvarez Bravo,
Los Obstaculos, 1929.
Gelatin silver print.
$6^{7}/_{8}$ x 9.
Courtesy Lunn Gallery
and the artist.

Ansel Adams,
St. Francis Church, Ranchos de Taos, New Mexico, c. 1929.
Silver print.
6 x 8½.
Courtesy the artist.

Adams made this extraordinarily sculptural photograph of the Ranchos de Taos church for the book *Taos Pueblo,* on which he collaborated with the writer Mary Austin. *Taos Pueblo* was published in San Francisco in 1930 by the Grabhorn Press in an edition of 108 deluxe copies. The twelve prints in the book are highly unusual, since, although they were made on the same wove paper that was used for the text, they are not reproductions printed with ink. The paper was sensitized with silver salts, and Adams printed on it directly from the negatives. The resulting matte prints look much like platinum prints. Its combination of images, text, printing, and binding makes *Taos Pueblo* one of the most beautiful of all photographic books.

Adams and Strand met in Taos in 1930, when both were staying at Mabel Dodge Luhan's colony of artists and writers. The story goes that when Adams saw some of Strand's negatives, he decided to give up his career as a concert pianist and devote himself entirely to photography.

Although Strand would surely have seen Adams's photograph in *Taos Pueblo* by the summer of 1931, when he made his own photograph of the church, he appears to have been more influenced by Georgia O'Keeffe's 1930 painting of the same subject than he was by Adams's photograph. Strand's image, with its cloudy sky and subtle modulations of light and dark, is as painterly as Adams's, with its blank sky and clearly defined highlights and shadows, is sculptural. Strand waited patiently for the right light for his photograph. When he saw a storm brewing, he rushed over from his house, which was about four miles away from the church, to make the photograph he had envisioned.

In 1937, Adams returned to the Ranchos de Taos church and made a photograph that looks like a homage to Strand's image. It is odd that this later and somewhat derivative photograph has become better known than the earlier and more personal one.

Paul Strand,
Church, Ranchos de Taos, New Mexico, 1931.
Gelatin silver print.
7 1/2 x 9 3/4.
Courtesy Sotheby's. © The Paul Strand Foundation.

Alexander Rodchenko,
Steps, 1930.
Gelatin silver print.
$10\,5/8$ x $15\,3/4$.
Private collection.

When Rodchenko made this photograph of a woman carrying her child and walking up a flight of stone steps, he must have remembered at some level the famous scene in Sergei Eisenstein's 1925 movie *The Battleship Potemkin* showing the Cossack massacre of civilians—including a woman with a child—on the steps leading down to the harbor of Odessa. Rodchenko knew Eisenstein and had designed several posters for *The Battleship Potemkin*—including one that reproduces a still from the scene on the steps. In that still, one can see the same graphic pattern of black-and-white stripes created by sunlight and shadow on the steps that one sees in Rodchenko's photograph. In the still, however, the steps are seen more or less straight on, and they are crowded with bodies and fleeing people. Rodchenko, characteristically, shot his photograph from above, composed his image with strong diagonals, and used the woman abstractly as an accent.

Although the Soviet government had been tolerant of avant-garde artists during the 1920s, it was well on the way to a policy of extreme repression by 1930. In 1929 the avant-garde magazine *New Left Front of the Arts,* which Rodchenko had helped

Ben Shahn,
Post Office, New York City,
c. 1933.
Gelatin silver print.
$6^{15}/_{16}$ x $9^{1}/_{16}$.
Fogg. Courtesy Mrs.
Bernarda Shahn.

to edit and which had published many of his photographs, ceased publication. All photographs without overt propagandistic value—and especially all photographs with tendencies toward abstraction—were officially condemned. Moreover, communication with the West was increasingly limited. It is, therefore, highly unlikely that Shahn could have seen Rodchenko's photograph, though he could possibly have seen Eisenstein's film, and he would certainly have been familiar—through Walker Evans—with the graphic design orientation in European photography.

In both his paintings and his photographs, however, Shahn was primarily interested in people. Although he took excellent advantage of the compositional opportunity offered by the steps, his main reason for making the photograph in the first place almost certainly had to do with the two girls who were rather precariously climbing the steps while wearing roller skates. When, in 1947, Shahn decided to base a painting on a photograph of East Twelfth Street that he had made in 1933, he lifted the two girls right out of his photograph of the post office steps and right on to the sidewalk in that painting.

As early as 1897, a book by Walter E. Woodbury entitled *Photographic Amusements* included sketches of trick photographs of scenes featuring what appear to be severed heads. The author explains that the images had been made by a Frenchman named Riccart using "a natural black background obtained through the open door of a dark room combined with diaphragms" inside the camera bellows.

Steichen's portrait of the actress Anna May Wong did not, then, involve a radical technical innovation—but it did involve a fairly radical artistic innovation, since Steichen daringly elevated a hobbyist's trick to the highest realm of professional portraiture. His photograph is explicable up to a point in terms of a high-collared black dress, meticulously controlled lighting, and virtuoso printing, and yet the portrait is ultimately so graceful, so beautiful, and so mysterious that it seems beside the point to analyze it.

When Steichen photographed Wong, he was at the peak of his commercial success. He was chief photographer for Condé Nast Publications; he had virtually everyone who had achieved national prominence in the arts and in politics clamor-

Cecil Beaton,
Charles James, 1936.
Gelatin silver print.
15 x 13½.
Courtesy Sotheby's.

ing for a chance to pose in front of his camera; and he was getting rich from advertising assignments. Steichen's portrait of Anna May Wong is clearly the work of a man who was very sure of himself.

Beaton was, in some respects, the English counterpart of Steichen. As one of the principal fashion and portrait photographers for Condé Nast in England, Beaton would surely have seen Steichen's portrait of Anna May Wong when it appeared in *Vanity Fair* in 1930. The Steichen may perhaps have inspired him to revive an idea he had used in 1924—when he photographed the heads of his two sisters and their reflections on the surface of a highly polished table. In keeping with his flamboyant personality and his preoccupation with highly theatrical and fantastic effects, he decided to push the illusion of decapitation to an extreme when he photographed fashion designer Charles James. The effect is even more bizarre than that of the Steichen, and yet Beaton took no special pains to conceal the mechanics of his trick. Perhaps Beaton couldn't resist introducing a note of modernistic, Brechtian anti-illusionism into his otherwise illusionistic image.

Walker Evans,
*Doorway, 204 West
Thirteenth Street,
New York,* c. 1931.
Gelatin silver print.
8 1/16 x 6 3/8.
Courtesy the Estate
of Walker Evans.

During 1930, after he had first seen reproductions of some of Atget's photographs, Evans shifted from the 35mm candid shots of people that he had been making for a year or so to large format photographs of buildings, windows, doors, signs, and whatever else caught his eye. He made his monolithic photograph of a Greek Revival doorway on West Thirteenth Street with a six- by eight-inch format, tripod-mounted view camera.

Abbott had had ample opportunity to become familiar with Evans's work by the time she photographed the same doorway. Evans had exhibitions of his work in 1932 and 1935 at Julien Levy's Gallery in New York, where he and Abbott were also included in a 1932 show entitled "Photographs of New York by New York Photographers." In 1933 Evans had a one-man show of photographs of nineteenth-century houses at the Museum of Modern Art. Although there is no record of whether Evans showed his photograph of the doorway in any of these exhibitions, it is certainly possible and—since it is one of his greatest photographs of that period— even likely that he did.

Abbott's documentation of New York architecture was as systematic as Evans's was eclectic. She photographed what she felt was historically important—especially if it seemed threatened by "progress." She was correct in her intuition that the doorway on West Thirteenth was endangered; it no longer exists. Abbott was evidently quite interested in Greek Revival doorways, for several photographs of them appear in her book *Changing New York*, published in 1939.

In order to convey as much information as possible about her subject, Abbott, who was of course also greatly influenced by Atget, kept her picture toward the middle range of grays, and she set up her eight- by ten-inch view camera far enough away from the doorway so that it could be seen in the context of the graceful railing and the classically proportioned window. Evans, however, zeroed in on the doorway itself and eliminated its setting, simultaneously focusing the viewer's attention on its magnificent detail and distilling the inherently enigmatic nature of closed doors. To heighten the effect of mystery, Evans made the noble but dingy doorway seem to emerge, like an apparition, out of the surrounding darkness.

Berenice Abbott,
Doorway, 204 West Thirteenth Street, New York, 1937.
Gelatin silver print.
$9^{3}/_{8}$ x $7^{5}/_{8}$.
MCNY.

Alexander Rodchenko,
Diver, 1932.
Gelatin silver print.
15 3/4 x 11 5/8.
Private collection.

After 1930, when the ideological waters in the Soviet Union became treacherous, Rodchenko mainly confined himself to the safe subjects of sports and construction. His high and low camera viewpoints and his fascination with semi-abstract patterns, which struck the censors as inappropriate for depictions of everyday life, were ideally suited to capturing the excitement of sports events and the precise patterns of mass athletic demonstrations.

Rodchenko photographed divers, from above and from below, on several occasions during the 1930s. In this extraordinary photograph of a diver doing a reverse tuck, Rodchenko used such an extreme upward angle that he eliminated all reference to the ground and showed the diver as if he were floating freely in the air, soaring above the clouds. (It has, however, been suggested that Rodchenko inverted his image after printing it.) The government, which placed great emphasis on sports, must have looked kindly on such depictions of superhuman athletic prowess. It is also possible that Rodchenko's photographs of divers were seen and admired by the

German filmmaker Leni Riefenstahl, who included some spectacular footage of divers seen from all angles in her film of the 1936 Berlin Olympics.

Erwitt, who has always responded with sharp wit and quick reflexes to the ways that people expose and disport themselves on the beach, had probably never seen Rodchenko's photograph. It is most likely that he simply saw what was happening as the boy began his flip and photographed it—without giving any thought to historical antecedents. It is thus probably only by coincidence that the suspended position of the boy in Erwitt's photograph corresponds exactly to the position of the man in one frame of Eadweard Muybridge's sequence of a man doing a back flip. Muybridge published his sequence in his book *Animal Locomotion* in 1887.

Rodchenko photographed his diver as heroic, but Erwitt photographed his boy as an enigma. Rodchenko's diver appears to have escaped from the range of gravity, but Erwitt's boy is very clearly within it. His suspension of gravity appears to astound the boy wading in the distance as much as it does the viewer.

Elliott Erwitt,
Saintes Maries de la Mer, France, 1977.
Gelatin silver print.
$9^1/_2$ x $6^5/_{16}$.
Courtesy Magnum.

Francis Bruguière,
New York, 1932.
Gelatin silver print.
$9^3/_8$ x $6^1/_4$.
Phillips.

Bruguière, who is known primarily for his photographic abstractions and his films, made this photograph of the buildings on East Fortieth Street between Park and Madison avenues in 1932 as a study for what he called a "pseudomorphic" film about New York. Before he moved to London in 1928, Bruguière had planned to collaborate with the industrial and theatrical designer Norman Bel Geddes on a series of short films about New York, but it wasn't until his visit to New York in 1932 that Bruguière actually began to photograph the city's architecture. No film ever materialized, but Bruguière did publish several of his photographs, including the one shown here, in the March 1933 issue of the British film magazine *Close Up.* Bruguière's accompanying stream-of-consciousness commentary makes it clear that his years in England had given him a cynical perspective on New York. He saw the city's skyscrapers as "pseudomorphs"—false forms, full of false optimism.

Bruguière's photograph, like the others in the series, juxtaposes the light and dramatically vertical form of a single skyscraper, photographed on a diagonal and

from a dizzying angle against the darker forms of smaller buildings in the middle ground and very dark, bold, and graphic forms in the foreground. According to Oswell Blakeston, who wrote about these New York photographs in *Close Up*, Bruguière's extreme camera angle was inspired by those in the films of Soviet director Dziga Vertov, who was in turn influenced by Rodchenko's photographs.

It is possible that Abbott may have seen Bruguière's photograph through their mutual friend Julien Levy, whose gallery presented Abbott's first New York show in 1932. Levy's great collection of photographs included many by Bruguière.

Like Bruguière, Abbott set up her camera close beside the south wall of the Murray Hill Hotel, which occupied the northwest corner of Park Avenue and East Fortieth Street, but she oriented the skyscraper vertically rather than diagonally, and she photographed it in more even—and less dramatic—light. Her treatment of the central group of buildings, which is still intact, is much more straightforward and documentary than Bruguière's.

Berenice Abbott,
Murray Hill Hotel: Spiral,
1935.
Gelatin silver print.
$9^{3}/_{4}$ x $7^{13}/_{16}$.
MCNY.

Brassaï took up photography in 1929, after having watched his friend André Kertész make long exposures on a dark night in Paris. Brassaï was fascinated by the night and had been searching for a way to record what he saw in the streets and the nightspots of the city.

For the next few years, Brassaï photographed incessantly at night—getting prostitutes, hoodlums, and other denizens of the night world to pose for his long exposures. He recorded scenes in brothels and nightclubs, at bizarre parties, and in the dark, almost deserted streets. It is appropriate that Brassaï included La Santé prison in his survey of nocturnal Paris, for many of his underworld subjects must have ended up there at one time or another. In 1933, Brassaï published the best of his photographs—including this one of La Santé—in his extraordinary book *Paris de Nuit (Paris at Night)*.

In that same year, Gisèle Freund fled from Berlin, where her student activities had got her in trouble with the Nazis, to Paris, where she enrolled in the graduate

school of the Sorbonne and wrote her dissertation on the sociology of nineteenth-century French photography. Freund's own photographic work divides itself into three major categories: color portraits of great French and English artists and writers, photojournalism, and her private portrait of Paris—to which her photograph of the wall of La Santé belongs.

Freund had long known both Brassaï and his book, and her photograph of La Santé was surely made by way of both homage and friendly competition. The perspectival effect of the wall is practically identical in both photographs, but otherwise they are almost polar opposites. The Brassaï, even though it was made at night, is quite brightly illuminated with an almost unearthly light from streetlamps outside the picture, which cast shadows of the bare trees onto the rough wall. The Freund, though it was made during the day, is dark with shadows cast by the wall and the densely foliated trees. Freund's photograph is an almost abstract composition in which all of the lines and the triangles they define converge dramatically at a single point.

Gisèle Freund,
Wall of La Santé Prison, 1974.
Gelatin silver print.
$11^3/_4$ x $7^7/_8$.
Courtesy Janis Gallery
and the artist.

Walker Evans,
*Bowery Restaurant,
New York,* c. 1933.
Gelatin silver print.
7¼ x 9⅛.
Courtesy Lunn Gallery
and the Estate of
Walker Evans.

In 1930, when Evans was prowling the streets of New York with a 35mm camera, he made a wonderful candid shot—taken from the sidewalk looking in—of people eating at the window counter of a lunchroom. In 1933, however, he was working with a view camera and making photographs devoid of people. By that time, his interest in signs and vernacular art had been stimulated by Atget, so it was probably the stylized painting of a fish that drew Evans's attention to this particular Bowery restaurant window. Evans photographed the window from a slightly oblique angle, apparently so that a reflection of him and his camera would not appear in the photograph. One can see Atget's reflection in many of his photographs of café facades, but Evans was an aloof and fastidious photographer who did not want to reveal his presence any more than was necessary. Ironically, it is Evans's posture of cool distance tempered with a wry appreciation of the naïve that most readily identifies this photograph as his.

The only place that Abbott could have seen Evans's photograph between 1933 and October 1935, when she made her own, was in his April 1935 show at Julien

Levy's gallery—if it was even included in that show. Abbott, however, probably just decided on her own that her survey of New York would not be complete without a Bowery lunchroom and proceeded to find one that looked interesting. The Blossom evidently won out because it was next door to a barbershop, so Abbott could show the prices of a meal and of a shave in a single picture. Furthermore, the barber's pole made a great compositional accent.

The most obvious difference between the Evans and the Abbott is that the latter includes two people. Furthermore, Abbott chose very neatly lettered and printed signs so that she could convey as much information about prices as possible. Evans seems to have been much less interested in documenting prices than in capturing a sense of the person who idiosyncratically painted the window.

Ben Shahn also photographed a Bowery restaurant window during the early 1930s. Typically, his image is dominated by two men whose gestures interested him, while much of the lettering on the window is arbitrarily cut off by the edge of the picture.

Berenice Abbott,
Blossom Restaurant,
103 Bowery, New York, 1935.
Gelatin silver print.
$6^{7}/_{8}$ x $8^{3}/_{4}$.
MCNY.

Alexander Rodchenko,
Girl with a Leica, 1934.
Gelatin silver print.
15³/₄ x 11¹/₂.
Private collection.

Girl with a Leica was a daringly abstract photograph for Rodchenko to make after having been severely criticized—by the Soviet censors and even by his doctrinaire colleagues—for his enduring interest in abstraction. In 1931 he had been expelled from the artistic group called October for "trying to divert proletarian art to the road of Western-style advertising, formalism, and aesthetics."

Rodchenko had been a brilliant abstract painter before he turned to photography around 1923—and the grid pattern in *Girl with a Leica* is strongly reminiscent of the grids and cross-hatching in some of his black-and-white drawings and linoleum cuts of 1918–19. When, in 1934 (the year of *Girl with a Leica*), Rodchenko wrote about the artistic potential of photography, he stressed that photographers should take advantage of the camera's propensity for "Contrasts of perspective. Light contrasts. Contrasts of forms. Viewpoints inaccessible to drawing or painting. . . . Compositions with an extremely complex play of lines." The second and the last of these elements are particularly evident in *Girl with a Leica.*

We may be quite certain that Evans had no way of seeing Rodchenko's photograph before 1947. It is, then, in at least one sense, purely coincidental that Rodchenko and Evans made such similar photographs of young women caught in the nets of light-and-shadow patterns formed by grilles. In another sense, however, patterns of light and shadow are such quintessentially photographic motifs that they have attracted photographers from Fox Talbot onward. *(See photographs by Talbot [page 40], Regnault [page 41], Weston [page 86], Man Ray [page 87], Rodchenko [pages 110 and 120], Umbo [page 111], Shahn [page 121], Abbott [page 150], Feininger [page 151], Laughlin [page 160], and White [page 161]).*

At the beginning of his career Evans had made some memorable photographs at Coney Island, and throughout the last thirty years of his life he occasionally returned to beaches to mine their rich lodes of the surreal. In his extraordinary photograph of Santa Monica, the effect of the light makes the girls in their bathing suits look as if they were walking on the bottom of a pool.

Walker Evans,
Santa Monica, California, 1947.
Gelatin silver print.
$6^3/_8$ x $6^1/_8$.
Courtesy Lunn Gallery and
the Estate of Walker Evans.

Walker Evans,
Window Display, Bethlehem,
Pennsylvania, 1935.
Gelatin silver print.
9⁹/₁₆ x 7³/₄.
LC.

Evans's photograph of a hardware store window belongs to the documentation of the steel-producing city of Bethlehem, Pennsylvania, that he made for the Resettlement Administration in November 1935. Evans focused on the city and its people rather than on the factories, but in some of the strongest pictures in the series, the smokestacks of the factories loom beyond the workers' houses and the gravestones in the local cemetery.

The merchandise displayed in the hardware store window adds up to an inventory of the necessities of domestic life. Evans's photograph is so packed with information that one could arrive by extrapolation from it at a fairly full, general conception of the material side of life in a typical Bethlehem household in 1935.

Since Evans did not include this photograph in his book *American Photographs,* it is unlikely that Strand had seen it. Even if Strand had known Evans's picture, he would probably not have felt that it had much to do with his own. At first, all that the photographs appear to have in common is the placement of the hanging brooms. On further inspection, however, one may see that the rug beater hanging to

the left of the broom in the Strand has a counterpart in the corresponding position in the Evans. And there are other compositional similarities: the windowsill in the Evans and the porch floor in the Strand, the reflection of trees at the top of the Evans and the glimpse of landscape beyond the open door in the Strand, the milk can in the lower right corner of the Evans and the metal can on the floor just inside the door in the Strand. Nevertheless, as similar as the compositions and some aspects of the subjects may be, the photographs reflect very different attitudes. Strand has expressed his reverence for the old-fashioned virtues and austerity of New England farm life, while Evans has expressed his ironic fascination with what others might see as the banality of modern life in a small Pennsylvania industrial city.

Strand made his photograph of the side porch for the book *Time in New England* on which he collaborated with the photographic historian Nancy Newhall. The tone of Strand's photographs is perfectly in keeping with that of the text, which is an anthology of writings by such New Englanders as Hawthorne, Melville, Emerson, Thoreau, and Emily Dickinson.

Paul Strand,
Side Porch, Vermont, 1947.
Gelatin silver print.
$8^3/_8$ x $5^{15}/_{16}$.
Courtesy Lunn Gallery.
© The Paul Strand
Foundation.

In his work for the Resettlement Administration and its successor, the Farm Security Administration, Lee made a specialty of photographs of people inside their homes. Evans, on the other hand, made a specialty of building exteriors. When he photographed interiors, he usually did not include any people. And when he photographed people, he usually did so on the street or on porches. The series of portraits of the sharecropper Bud Fields and his family that he made in Alabama in the summer of 1936 and the photograph of a miner's son reproduced here are among the very few exceptions. Lee could easily have seen Evans's photograph in the RA files, but whether or not it actually influenced him is entirely another matter.

Evans virtually always used the available natural light to illuminate his subjects. In his photograph of the miner's son, he seated the boy so that the light from a window or a doorway streamed onto him from outside the left edge of the picture, giving him an uncannily angelic glow. Lee, however, generally used a flash attached to his camera to illuminate interiors. The bright, harsh light of his flash is clearly evident in his photograph of the sharecropper's son, for it glares on the bureau and

on the newspapers with which the walls were covered to keep out drafts.

Evans, who was drawn to the surreal effects created by pictorial signs, must have delighted in the array of advertising images pasted onto the wall of the cabin. Because of the boy's celestial-seeming radiance, the two women and the Santa Claus seem like divine protectors watching over him. And yet, since the boy has probably never got much for Christmas, the Santa Claus gives the photograph the kind of irony that one finds in Dorothea Lange's 1938 photograph of two migrant workers walking past a billboard that reads, "Next Time Try the Train—Relax."

The boy in Evans's photograph, who is sitting on one half of his chair and staring rather blankly at the camera, looks as if he were intimidated by Evans's presence. Evans was, after all, an uncompromising artist, who used a cumbersome and imposing eight- by ten-inch tripod-mounted view camera with a black cloth that went over his head while focusing. Lee, however, used a much less conspicuous hand-held four- by five-inch plate camera and was known for his ability to put people at ease. The boy in his picture looks totally absorbed in his grooming.

Russell Lee,
Sharecropper's Son,
Missouri, 1938.
Gelatin silver print.
$7^1/_4$ x $9^3/_8$.
LC.

Soon after Lange turned from studio portraiture to documentary photography, about 1933, her work came to the attention of economist Paul Taylor, who was writing extensively on the problems of migrant agricultural laborers in California and the Southwest. Taylor realized that Lange could make the photographs he needed to dramatize the facts and statistics in his reports. He hired Lange in 1934, and together they traveled throughout California documenting the working and living conditions of migrants.

In the spring of 1935, they issued a report in a limited number of typed copies with prints of Lange's photographs pasted in. Since the migrant families traveled from one labor camp to another by car, many of Lange's photographs focus on destitute, desperate people in their battered automobiles.

That summer, Shahn, who was then gaining a reputation as a painter dealing with social issues, was hired as an artist—not as a photographer—by the Special Skills Section of the Resettlement Administration. Shahn was to make posters and murals for the RA, but he soon began to use his photographic skills to document the

poverty that the RA was to combat. As a fellow employee of the RA, Shahn was present when Roy Stryker, head of the RA's Historical Section, first saw a copy of the Taylor-Lange report. Shahn later recalled that Lange's photographs came as nothing short of a revelation to him. They also had a great impact on Stryker, who soon decided that his section should be devoted to a massive documentary photographic project. He then hired Lange and Walker Evans, among others, and sent Shahn on a long trip, in the fall of 1935, through the Southeast.

Although Shahn may or may not have seen *Ditched, Stalled, and Stranded* (since it is unclear exactly when in 1935 Lange made her photograph), he had certainly seen many Lange photographs of similar subjects before he set out on his trip. Shahn's choice of subject reflects Lange's influence, but his handling of it is very much his own. Shahn's image is almost cubistic in its visual complexity, while Lange's is direct and to the point. Shahn's photograph, for all its documentary impact, was made from the standpoint of a painter, while Lange's, for all its richness as a work of art, was made by a dedicated documentarian.

Dorothea Lange,
Ditched, Stalled, and Stranded, San Joaquin Valley, California, 1935. Gelatin silver print. 8 5/16 x 7 5/8. LC.

Ben Shahn,
Rehabilitation Clients,
Boone County, Arkansas,
1935.
Gelatin silver print.
6¹/₂ x 9⁹/₁₆.
LC.

Shahn made a whole series of photographs of this desperate- and bewildered-looking woman, who throughout the series stands in front of her cabin and keeps her arms crossed in front of her. In some of the pictures, she looks almost as if she were shivering from the cold, but in the photograph reproduced here she is making a gesture that seems to symbolize confusion, worry, fatigue, and self-defense from the prying eye of the camera, all at the same time. Her daughter, leaning against the doorpost, looks as if she is the one who keeps the family going.

Lange may have seen Shahn's photograph in the Resettlement Administration files when, in December 1936, she made the first of her infrequent trips to Washington. All of the RA photographers except Lange, who was based in San Francisco, returned to Washington between assignments to study the office's photographic files and to confer with their boss, Roy Stryker, about the gaps that needed to be filled in. Lange usually kept in touch by mail, sending her negatives to Washington and receiving instructions—sometimes very specific and detailed—from Stryker about what kind of photographs he needed. Perhaps because she was so far away from

Washington, Lange was one of the photographers to be laid off when the RA became the Farm Security Administration in 1937. She then decided to continue her documentary work by collaborating with Paul Taylor, whom she had married in 1935, on a book about farmers and migrant agricultural workers in the South and the Southwest. Although she was not employed by the FSA, she sold many negatives to the agency for its files.

Lange photographed the "woman of the high plains" in Childress County, Texas, in June 1938, near the beginning of the trip on which she made most of the photographs for her book *An American Exodus*. Lange's two great motifs of the 1930s were migrants in their cars and strong, determined, but destitute women. The "woman of the high plains" looks tough, resilient, and intelligent, but also hot and tired. Lange has photographed her from a low angle so that she stands tall against the sky. It was the optimism of this compositional strategy, as well as the graphic simplicity of the single figure, that transformed this image, like so many others by Lange, from the picture of an admirable individual into a symbol of the time.

Dorothea Lange,
Woman of the High Plains,
Texas Panhandle, 1938.
Gelatin silver print.
$9^{3}/_{4}$ x $7^{1}/_{2}$.
OM.

Evans made his photograph in March 1936, when he was in Mississippi documenting soil erosion for the Resettlement Administration. It is an anomaly in his oeuvre,
for Evans generally showed little interest in landscape. Most of his work for the RA
consists of close-up "portraits" of individual buildings, photographs of signs and
monuments, and pictures of people. But Evans liked this photograph well enough to
include it in his book *American Photographs,* published in the fall of 1938 to accompany a major exhibition of his work at the Museum of Modern Art in New York.
Although Lange had already made her photograph by the time Evans's book appeared, she could have seen the image in the RA files when she was in Washington
in December 1936.

Lange shot *Tractored Out* in June 1938, in the same county in which she photographed the "woman of the high plains" *(see page 143). Tractored Out* is a key
image in *An American Exodus,* for it illustrates the central thesis that large-scale,
mechanized farming was displacing thousands upon thousands of small farmers.
Paul Taylor's caption for the photograph reads, "Tractors replace not only mules,

but people. They cultivate to the very door of the houses of those whom they replace."

There are several rather similar photographs of tractored farms in *An American Exodus,* but *Tractored Out* is the strongest, for its furrows, which converge on the house, pull the viewer's eye into the picture and straight to the abandoned house. In contrast to the stark, unrelieved barrenness recorded in Lange's image—which is as graphically bold as a poster—Evans's very atypically cropped photograph, made with an eight- by ten-inch plate camera, is delicate and lyrical, as well it should be. Although it may look at first as if Evans and Lange were both documenting the same phenomenon, the farm that Evans photographed was still very much inhabited—and the field was presumably plowed with mule-power. If one looks carefully enough, one can see people on the porch on the left side of the house, as well as two children to the right of the house—one hugging the wall and the other playing on the woodpile. There's also laundry on the line out back and a tree house in the tree at the center.

Dorothea Lange,
Tractored Out, Childress County, Texas, 1938.
Gelatin silver print.
7 x 9¹/₂.
LC.

Walker Evans,
Atlanta, Georgia, 1936.
Gelatin silver print.
7⅝ x 9⅜.
LC.

At first glance, the two houses in Evans's photograph appear to be identical. Only after further inspection does one begin to notice the differences. The house on the left has curtains at its upstairs window, while that on the right does not. The porch of the house on the left extends almost all the way across the facade, while the porch of the house on the right stops approximately where it is intersected by the telephone pole. The house on the left has a washing basin on its upstairs porch, while what may be the basin from the house on the right is out on the curb—upside down and with its bottom smashed in. The arrangement of drainpipes and the patterns surrounding the oval openings of the porches also differ.

It appears that Evans playfully emphasized the parallels between the oval porch screen of the relatively comfortable-looking house on the left and the shape of the chair pictured on the billboard in front of it and between the corresponding oval of the barren house on the right and Carole Lombard's black eye.

In 1936 John Vachon began working as a file clerk for the Resettlement Administration, for which Evans made his photograph. He said later that he knew Evans's photograph and that when he found himself in Atlanta in 1938, by which time he was a photographer himself, he hired a cab to drive him all over the city to look for Evans's houses. When he found them, he framed his picture differently, using the telephone pole to mark the right edge of his composition. Paraphrasing Evans's comparison between the houses and the billboards, Vachon apparently focused on the features of Robert Donat in the *Count of Monte Cristo* poster and composed his picture so that the shape of the sky above and between the houses made a visual pun on Donat's forehead and nose. The two porch ovals then became compositional equivalents of Donat's eyes, while the telephone wire echoes his high eyebrows. Vachon may thus have made a droll homage to Evans's witty and yet monumental photograph.

John Vachon,
Atlanta, Georgia, 1938.
Gelatin silver print.
7¹/₈ x 9¹/₈.
LC.

Walker Evans,
Tin Building, Moundville,
Alabama, 1936.
Gelatin silver print.
6³/₈ x 9.
LC.

Ever since the time of Talbot and Daguerre, photography and painting have been engaged in a game of leapfrog in which each medium has successively expanded the other's boundaries of style and content. Walker Evans's choice of subject matter, for instance, was surely influenced to some extent by the work of contemporary Precisionist artists—including painter/photographer Charles Sheeler—many of whom frequently depicted barns and factories. The terse, factual, and direct "portraits" of building facades that Evans made in the American South in 1936 were, however, in marked contrast to the Precisionists' cubistically faceted and "artistic" treatments of similar subjects. Evans's photographs were not widely appreciated until the Minimalist art of the 1960s had made virtues of their austerity, literalness, symmetry, and frontality.

Although Evans's unpeopled architectural images are now considered to be among his strongest photographs, Evans himself apparently did not originally perceive them as such, for he included no images in *American Photographs* that are simultaneously as spare, as devoid of people, as anti-picturesque, and as abstract as is that of the shed housing Richard Perkins's contracting business in Moundville,

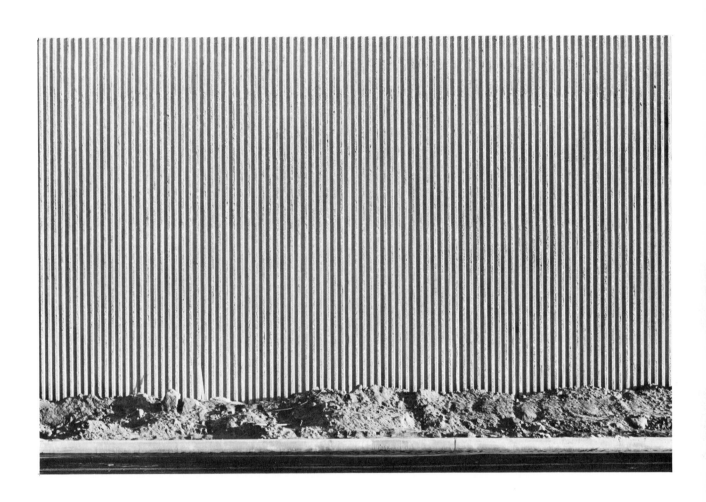

Lewis Baltz,
West Wall, Unoccupied Industrial Structure, c. 1974. Gelatin silver print. 6 x 9. Coll. Marvin Heiferman. Courtesy Castelli Photograph and the artist.

Alabama. Baltz had known and admired *American Photographs* ever since it had been reissued in 1962, but by about 1970 Minimalist painting and sculpture seemed more relevant to Baltz's concerns than did most photographs—even Evans's. Baltz has stated that it was only when the Perkins shed photograph and several others in a related vein were published in the catalog of Evans's 1971 retrospective at the Museum of Modern Art that he came to see how Evans related directly to the aesthetics of Minimalism.

Evans photographed the entire facade of the Perkins shed and enough of its surroundings to convey a sense of place. He also recorded a play of light and shadow as tonally rich, in its way, as that in Paul Strand's photograph of the Ranchos de Taos church *(see page 119)*. Indeed, the Evans is like a flattened-out, deromanticized version of the Strand. Baltz has continued the flattening and abstracting process to such an extent that only the narrow band of earth and concrete at the bottom of the photograph prevents the striped pattern of the wall—which alludes to such Minimalist work as Daniel Buren's vertically striped wallpaper—from merging visually with the flat surface of the photograph itself.

Abbott's photograph is an atmospheric evocation of an old section of New York, where the streets were still paved with cobblestones—whose shapes are echoed by the patterns of light and shadow created by the structure of the elevated tracks. As in many of her photographs of New York, Abbott has included people in the foreground both to give a sense of the city as "lived in" and to establish scale. This photograph was published in Abbott's book *Changing New York* in 1939. In her caption, Elizabeth McCausland wrote that the El's lease would not expire until 2878, "and no doubt by then all the 'Els' will be torn down." They were, in fact, torn down only a few years after Abbott photographed them. Her intuition that they should be included in her inventory of disappearing New York was correct.

It was in 1939 that Andreas Feininger immigrated to the United States. During

the 1920s, he had studied at the Bauhaus, taught himself photography, and worked as an architect in Germany. In the late 1930s, he worked as an architectural and industrial photographer in Sweden. Upon his arrival in the United States, Feininger began to work as a photojournalist. During the 1940s and 1950s, Feininger photographed many of the sites that Abbott had photographed earlier and published in her book, with which he was surely familiar. Feininger's picture of the El, taken from a spot several yards to the left and forward of where Abbott had stood, reflects the design sensibility of the Bauhaus in its emphasis on patterns of light and shadow forming a jazzy, modernistic abstraction. In order to reveal the structure and light patterns of the overhead tracks, Feininger positioned his camera somewhat lower than Abbott had positioned hers, and he aimed slightly upward.

Andreas Feininger,
Division Street, Second Avenue Elevated, 1941.
Gelatin silver print.
14 x 10³/₄.
ICP. Courtesy the artist.

Berenice Abbott,
Gunsmith's Sign and Police
Department, New York, 1937.
Gelatin silver print.
7³/₈ x 9³/₁₆.
MCNY.

The striking realism of the huge replica of a gun in Abbott's photograph paradoxically gives her image a surreal quality that is rarely seen in her work. Only the presence of the sign hanging from it betrays the fact that the gun is not a real one enlarged out of scale by being photographed in extreme close-up. It is especially ironic that the gun is pointing, as in a holdup, at a banklike building that was actually the headquarters for the New York City Police Department.

Abbott met Atget while she was living in Paris in the 1920s, and it was she who first fully appreciated his genius. After his death in 1927, she rescued his work from oblivion and set about to publish and exhibit it. When she returned to New York in 1929, she was inspired by Atget's legacy to make a survey of New York analogous to his grand inventory of the beauties and curiosities of Paris. Although the influence of Atget runs through all of Abbott's New York images, her photograph of the gunsmith's sign is one of the few that looks like a photograph that Atget could have made if he had ever visited New York. Abbott's vision of New York—in keeping with the spirit of the city—was usually harsher, less poetic, and less surreal than was Atget's depiction of Paris.

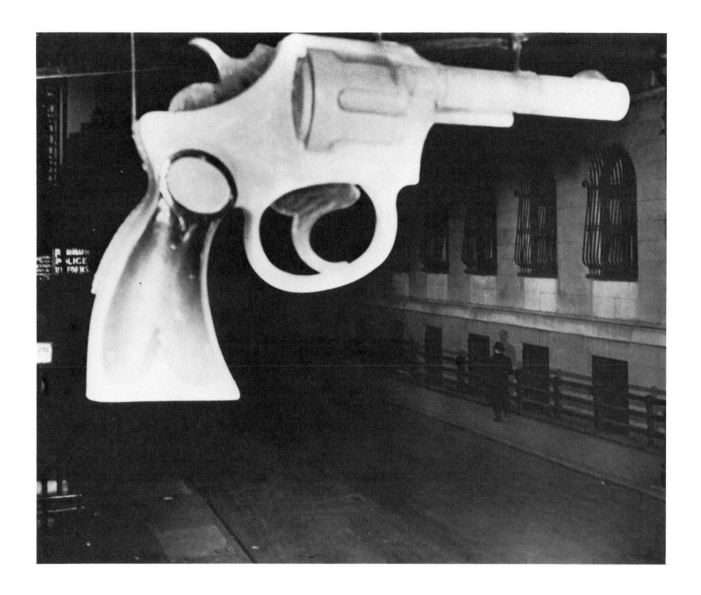

Weegee (Arthur Fellig),
Gun Shop, 1943.
Gelatin silver print.
9¹/₈ x 11³/₄.
ICP. Courtesy Mrs. Wilma
Wilcox.

Weegee, who could have seen Abbott's photograph in her 1939 book *Changing New York*, earned his nickname (derived from the Ouija board used in telling fortunes) because he had an uncanny knack for being the first photographer to show up at scenes of crime and disaster. As a free-lance photographer whose pictures were published in all the New York tabloids, Weegee made photographs that were extremely sensationalistic. Since many of the events he covered occurred at night, he became a master of using flashbulbs to reveal lurid details and to create a jarring, garish effect.

Weegee's photograph of a gunsmith's sign is one of his very few photographs in which people play a minor role. And yet, the harshly flash-lighted sign symbolizes his work so well that Weegee could have used this image as his logo. All the violence that he photographed is implicit in that menacing form hanging over the street.

Weegee did not photograph the same sign that Abbott had photographed—there were many gun stores around police headquarters—but Andreas Feininger did in the early 1940s. He chose to photograph Frank Lava's sign from an angle that eliminated the police building from his picture.

Dorothea Lange,
The Road West,
New Mexico, 1938.
Gelatin silver print.
6³⁄₈ x 9¹⁄₂.
OM.

Even though there are no people in it, Lange's photograph of U.S. 54 in southern New Mexico is one of the most powerful images of migration in her book *An American Exodus.* Her photograph of the route taken by so many who left the Oklahoma and Texas dust bowl for California captures the relentless pull of the road, which stretches off into the remote distance. The land on both sides of the road, as far as the eye can see, is dark and barren. Only the road itself is bright—a metaphor for hope. The road seems to veer upward at the straight horizon, as if it led up to the heavens. Lange may have intended this illusion as a comment on the hopes of the migrants, who expected to find a verdant paradise in California.

Frank was certainly aware of Lange's photograph when he made his own version of *The Road West.* In preparation for his trip across the United States in 1955–56, supported by a Guggenheim fellowship, he had studied the books of others who documented the American scene. Lange's book and Walker Evans's *American Photographs* were clearly among his richest sources of inspiration.

As in *An American Exodus*, roads and automobiles play an important role in Frank's book *The Americans*, which was published in France in 1958 and in the United States in 1959. But while the battered cars and long roads in Lange's photographs are simply the means to an end, the cars and roads in Frank's photographs are seen as ends in themselves.

The most obvious of the compositional differences between the Lange and the Frank is that of framing; the former is horizontal, stressing the relationship between the road and the land through which it passes, while the latter is vertical, stressing the road itself. The vanishing point of Lange's road is dead center, while that of Frank's is well to the left of center. Lange's road leads to a bright but blank sky, while Frank's leads to a dark, lowering sky. But the most momentous difference between the photographs is that while Lange's includes no cars, Frank's shows a car approaching the photographer. Lange photographed a symbol; Frank photographed an event.

Robert Frank,
U.S. 285, New Mexico,
1955–56.
Gelatin silver print.
13$\frac{1}{4}$ x 8$\frac{7}{8}$.
Coll. Susan H. Hager.
Courtesy Lunn Gallery.
© Robert Frank.

Edward Weston,
Rubber Dummies, M.G.M.
Lot, Culver City,
California, 1939.
Gelatin silver print.
7½ x 9½.
MoMA, gift of Edward
Steichen. Courtesy Cole
Weston.

In 1937 Weston became the first photographer ever to be awarded a Guggenheim fellowship. Although the money gave him the freedom to travel and to photograph extensively throughout California and the Southwest, and although he had just married a beautiful young woman named Charis Wilson, Weston's photographs from 1937 onward are far from lighthearted or optimistic. Of his first year on the fellowship (which was renewed in 1938), Weston wrote, "1300 negatives—21,000 miles of searching. No, I have not done 'faces and postures,' except one dead man (wish I could have found more) and many dead animals; but I have done ruins and wreckage by the square mile and square inch, and some satires."

The darkness of Weston's work of this time evidently derived, at least partially, from his sense that his richest creative period, which had lasted from about 1927 to 1937, was over. By 1937 he had exhausted the potential of his great series of nudes, clouds, peppers, cabbages, shells, and sand dunes. He was in his early fifties, and he clearly had a growing preoccupation with death. Perhaps he sensed that within ten years Parkinson's disease would put an end to his photographic career. Furthermore, the threat of war was in the air.

156

Weston's photograph of rubber dummies that were used in filming dangerous stunts is one of his most morbid and bitterly satiric photographs of the late 1930s. The standing dummies are grotesque parodies of men—empty shells with unseeing eyes, false muscles, disproportionately long arms, and no genitals. Others like them have been thrown carelessly onto the shelf behind, while the garbage can seems ready to receive any dummies that have worn out. The photograph is as angry and as ironic a reflection on the human condition as is any soliloquy in a Shakespearean tragedy.

Weston and Adams were close friends, and it is safe to assume that Adams had seen Weston's photograph before he visited the Columbia lot. Influenced by Weston's more or less surrealistic photographs, Adams made some wonderful images in a related vein during 1939 and 1940, before beginning to devote himself exclusively to landscape. But Adams was in the middle of his most creative period, and his photograph of mannequins is as optimistic as Weston's is pessimistic. In the Adams the mannequins, torsos, and arms, highlighted by bright sunlight, stand out from the fascinating clutter as if they were spare parts for angels.

Ansel Adams,
Mannequins, Columbia Movie Lot, Los Angeles, c. 1940.
Gelatin silver print.
13 1/8 x 19.
Courtesy the artist.

Robert Frank,
Chair, Paris, 1949.
Gelatin silver print.
13 x 8⁹/₁₆.
MoMA.
© Robert Frank.

When Frank photographed in Paris in 1949 and 1950, he had not yet come under the influence of Walker Evans's work. His chief hero at that time was André Kertész, and it is to Kertész that Frank was clearly paying a very droll homage in his photograph of a folding chair in the Tuileries Gardens. Kertész had made numerous gently witty photographs of such chairs, their shadows, and their occupants, but Frank went beyond wit to comedy. His photograph is an elegant and sophisticated joke that operates on several levels.

First of all, the chair is a parody of itself. It can just barely manage to stand up, but if anyone were to try to sit on it, the comedy would become slapstick. The chair is also vaguely anthropomorphic; it looks a little like a nightclub cigarette vendor with a big, square tray. Or it might suggest a strange creature scuttling across the barren, shadowless surface of the moon—for there is not a hint of context in the picture unless one recognizes the chair and knows that most of the Tuileries Gar-

dens is bare, hard-packed, pebble-covered earth. Frank first published his photograph in his book *The Lines of My Hand* in 1972.

While the humor in Frank's photograph is as finely tuned as a gesture in one of the comic films that Jacques Tati was just beginning to make in Paris at that time, the humor in Erwitt's photograph is broad and hearty. Erwitt, who is always quick to catch hopelessly awkward predicaments, has discovered the famous chairs—symbols of Paris's simple pleasures and civilized charm—in a state of total and humiliating collapse in a mud puddle.

Erwitt, who was born in France and who has made some of his funniest and most sensitive photographs in that country, is a photographic humorist on a par with such literary humorists as S. J. Perelman or Evelyn Waugh. Erwitt's photographs puckishly straddle the elusive boundary between the breakdown of normality that we call comedy and the intensified perception of form and meaning that we call art.

Elliott Erwitt,
Paris, 1969.
Gelatin silver print.
$5^{1}/_{4}$ x $7^{3}/_{4}$.
Courtesy Magnum.

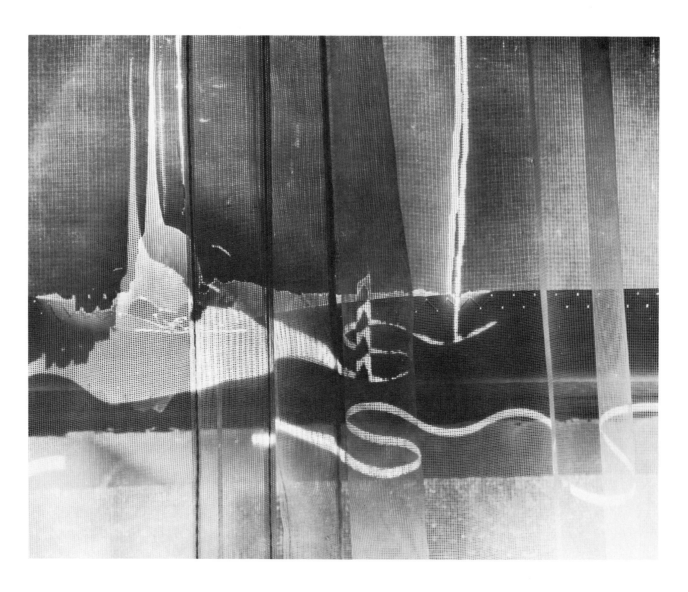

Since 1935, Laughlin, a romanticist inspired by the poetry of Baudelaire and Rim-
baud, has worked on twenty-three ongoing series of photographs, which have such
titles as "Fantasy in Old New Orleans," "Poems of the Inner World," and "The
Magic of the Object." *The Language of Light* belongs to the series entitled "The
Mystery of Space." Laughlin, who started out as a writer and who still conceives of
his captions as integral parts of his work, has written about this photograph: "What
we see is sunlight falling through a torn and carefully adjusted curtain, onto an old
wire screen. But space multiplies, and the light-forms begin to exist *independently of
the objects which helped to create them.* This is an example not only of how space can
be expanded by the camera, but also of the translation of the concrete into the
abstract, and finally, of the pure magic of light itself." It appears that the light is
actually coming through a wire screen and a torn shade onto a gauzy curtain.

It seems most likely that temperamental affinity with Laughlin rather than direct

influence from him led Minor White to make *Windowsill Daydreaming*, since *The Language of Light* was not published until later. Like Laughlin, White had a metaphysical turn of mind. He also began as a writer, divided his work into groups (which he called "sequences"), and wrote extensively about his photographs. *Windowsill Daydreaming* belongs to the sequence entitled "The Sound of One Hand Clapping." Most of the other photographs in the sequence are semi-abstract images of frost on the windows of White's Rochester apartment, where he made *Windowsill Daydreaming* in July 1958. White apparently conceived of these images as visual equivalents of sounds.

Laughlin's photograph, which excludes all reference to the window's frame, seems at first to be more purely abstract than White's, which makes the situation explicit. The light patterns in Laughlin's photograph, however, are more easily analyzed and explained than those in White's, which have no visible source.

Minor White,
Windowsill Daydreaming, 1958.
Gelatin silver print.
10³/₄ x 8⁷/₈.
Phillips. Courtesy MWA.
© The Trustees of Princeton University.

When Cartier-Bresson first took up photography in 1932, it was the work of Kertész, more than that of any other photographer, that made him aware of the agility of the 35mm Leica as a recorder of fleeting moments, as a tool for transcribing the poetry of human gestures. Cartier-Bresson has gone so far as to call Kertész his "poetic source." The two men are, nevertheless, fundamentally different, for Kertész is, above all else, a man of tender sentiment, while Cartier-Bresson is a man of penetrating intellect—and their photographs clearly reflect this difference. Futhermore, Kertész's sense of composition is quintessentially photographic, while Cartier-Bresson has learned more about composition from Renaissance painters than from other photographers. What the two men have most in common is their sensitivity to gesture, their sharp wit, and their sense of the surreal undercurrents in everyday life.

In the Kertész photograph reproduced here, the boy seems to be sealed off from the life that goes on around him as he performs a private and mysterious rite. His only contact with the outside world is with the photographer, whom he regards with pro-

found suspicion. It is probably only coincidental that this photograph, made in Mexico, is reminiscent of Manuel Alvarez Bravo's 1931 photograph entitled *The Dreamer,* in which a young Mexican man, clothed, in a position similar to that of Kertész's boy—though he has his left hand between his legs—is sleeping on a stone ledge.

Despite the obvious architectural similarities, the languorous boys, the out-stretched arms, and the sense of oppressive heat that the Kertész and the Cartier-Bresson have in common, the two photographs feel very different. In the Kertész, the boy overwhelms everything else. Spontaneous emotional response to his enig-matic gesture is primary; composition seems only secondary. In the Cartier-Bresson, the extraordinary balance of the composition is paramount. One may almost feel that Cartier-Bresson, who would never actually pose his subjects, has *willed* them into a composition that bears an uncanny resemblance to Giotto's fresco in the Arena Chapel in Padua depicting the scene in which the risen Christ tells Mary Magdalene not to touch him.

Henri Cartier-Bresson,
Simiane la Rotonde, 1970.
Gelatin silver print.
6¹/₂ x 9³/₄.
Courtesy Magnum.

Robert Frank,
Untitled, 1955–56.
Gelatin silver print.
9 x 13½.
Courtesy Lunn Gallery.
© Robert Frank.

During 1955 and 1956, when his Guggenheim fellowship enabled him to travel extensively around the United States, Frank exposed over 28,000 negatives, prints from only 83 of which eventually made it into his book *The Americans.* The photograph reproduced here was one of the thousands that ended up on the cutting-room floor. Several elements, however, connect it strongly with images that Frank chose to publish. There are two photographs in *The Americans* in which one of the subjects twists around to look at the photographer with hostility, and more than half a dozen that focus on people in parked or moving cars. Furthermore, the photograph of people in a convertible graphically illustrates the mood that beat poet Jack Kerouac described in the opening phrase of his introduction to *The Americans:* "That crazy feeling in America when the sun is hot on the streets . . ."

For Frank, cars are symbols of violence and isolation—both of which figure in the photograph of the convertible. The woman is so angry at Frank's intrusion that she is at the point of violence. This interaction between the anonymous woman and the photographer constitutes an ironic reference to paparazzi shots of celebrities. Frank

has played with this allusion to tabloid journalism by framing his image so that it looks as if he—like an overeager newspaper photographer—has actually scrambled up onto the car's trunk lid. The visual evidence suggests that Frank used a wider angle lens than did Winogrand.

Winogrand has frequently acknowledged that he has learned much from Frank, but it is unlikely that he could have seen this unpublished photograph by 1959— and, in any case, he had already been working in a style related to Frank's but not influenced by it for several years before Frank's book appeared. Both men had come under the spell of Walker Evans about 1955.

The monkey in Winogrand's photograph prefigures the many monkeys and other animals that Winogrand photographed in New York City zoos during the 1960s and published in a book that he entitled—apparently in mischievous homage to Frank's book—*The Animals*. Winogrand's photograph has all the black humor, sense of danger, quick response to gesture, and wry juxtaposition of people and animals that have led some critics to compare him with Goya.

Garry Winogrand,
New York, 1959.
Gelatin silver print.
13½ x 8¾.
MoMA. Courtesy the artist.

During the summer of 1938, Evans made a documentation of Sixty-first Street between First and Third avenues in New York City for the Farm Security Administration, which, despite its name, commissioned photographs of cities as well as of farms for its files. Evans used a 35mm camera for this project, as he had for some of his earliest New York work and for some of the photographs he had made in the South in the mid-1930s for the Resettlement Administration, which became the FSA in the fall of 1937.

In 1959 Evans returned to Third Avenue to make another 35mm documentation. It is uncertain whether he did so for a projected but never published *Fortune* essay or simply for his own pleasure. In either case, when Evans came across this lone brownstone, holding out against the wrecker's ball after its neighbors had all succumbed, he must have remembered a very similar scene that he had photographed for a photo-essay on Chicago that appeared in *Fortune* in February 1947. He had framed his picture of the Chicago house to include the whole building, standing alone against the background of a huge warehouse.

Evans's New York photograph, in his characteristic 35mm style, cuts off part of the subject. If he had been primarily interested in the house itself, he could have framed his image vertically, but he clearly wanted to show how isolated the house was. He therefore framed his image horizontally and included only as much of the house as was needed to make the point.

Kertész, who had not seen Evans's photograph, focused on the house, which had been abandoned and vandalized since Evans had photographed it. While Evans's photograph celebrates the house's pluckiness, Kertész's shows a doomed wreck. The ominous black limousine parked in front may even belong to the developer who succeeded in breaking down the old owner's resistance.

Kertész arrived in New York in 1936 with high hopes, but he found only unimaginative editors. The outbreak of war prevented him from returning to his beloved Paris. So he was forced to stay and photograph fashions and interiors that did not interest him. It is no wonder that in some of his New York photographs bitterness cuts through his usual gentle wit.

André Kertész,
New York, 1960.
Gelatin silver print.
10 x 7³/₄.
© André Kertész.

Lewis Baltz,
Unoccupied Warehouse,
Santa Ana, c. 1974.
Gelatin silver print. 6 x 9.
Courtesy Castelli Photo-
graphs and the artist.

Just as Moholy-Nagy discovered in the midst of the most casual events of life compositions like those of Malevich's rarefied, abstract paintings *(see pages 96 and 98),* so have Baltz and Mudford discovered in the most banal structures in the American landscape the modular, geometric forms of Minimalist art.

Baltz has isolated a section of a facade that presumably extends far beyond both sides of the picture and has created an image that again reflects the influence of Evans's photograph of the Perkins shed *(see page 148).* Evans's 1971 retrospective and its catalog did much to foster among young photographers a revival of interest in large format cameras. During the 1950s and 1960s, most young photographers who thought of themselves as artists used 35mm cameras, following the example first of Henri Cartier-Bresson and then of Robert Frank. Baltz was among those who turned to the eight by ten camera in the early 1970s. His work embodies the extreme clarity of focus made possible by the large screen of a view camera and by contact prints, which do not show any loss of detail or sharpness from negative to print. Mudford, in contrast, likes the graininess of enlargements from 35mm nega-

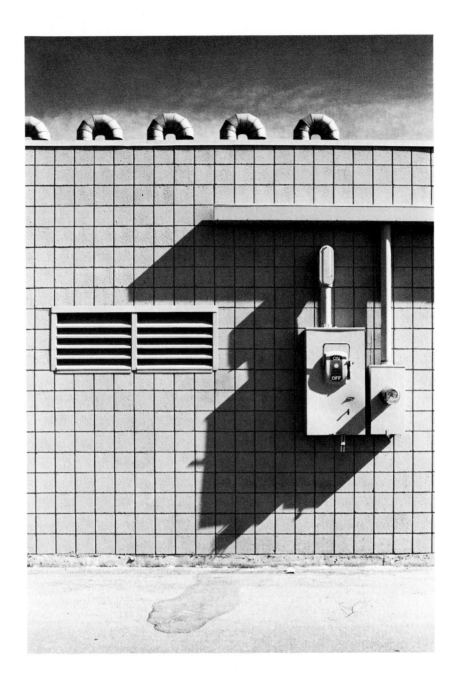

tives—reflecting his great admiration for the work of Bill Brandt *(see page 115)*.

Both the Baltz and the Mudford are frontal, airless, and unpopulated; and both focus on an isolated and interrupted pattern of square tiles. But the moods of the two photographs are very different. The Baltz is cool, elegant, deadpan, and ironic—for it is a magnificent photograph (as tonally rich and supple as a vintage print by Strand or Weston) of a markedly less than magnificent subject. It clearly alludes to the grid paintings that formed an important category of Minimalist art. But Baltz was interested in more than pattern here, for he photographed the facade in over-head light that accentuated the dents (caused by stacking during shipment) that come through from the back of the lightweight metal doors. Baltz has stated that he is drawn to photographing things that show very slight damage, that have evolved through use or abuse. Mudford, who characteristically made his photograph in very bright sunlight, seems to have been especially interested in the rather surreal relationship between the large, ominous shadow on the wall and the stain on the ground. His photograph has a distinct note of science-fiction drama.

NOTES ON PHOTOGRAPHIC PROCESSES

Processes are discussed in the order in which they came into general use.

The reader should bear in mind that many of the characteristics noted here will not be visible in the halftone reproductions in this book, for halftones translate all tones and textures into uniform patterns of black and white dots.

Daguerreotype

The daguerreotype process, announced in 1839, produced—without the intervention of a negative—a positive image on a highly reflective, silvered copper plate. To make a daguerreotype, the photographer fumed the plate with iodine vapor, which reacted with the silver to form light-sensitive silver iodide. After exposure in a camera, the image was developed with mercury vapor.

Because daguerreotypes were extremely susceptible to scratching, smearing, and tarnishing, they were usually kept sealed behind glass in small protective cases. After 1840, the developed and fixed plate was generally toned in a solution of gold chloride, which gave the image a rich purplish-brown cast and made it somewhat more resistant to damage—but daguerreotypes remained very fragile. Since a daguerreotype has a mirrored surface, the image cannot be seen clearly if one looks at it directly. One must find an oblique angle at which the light allows the image to become fully visible.

Daguerreotypy was the only photographic process that was widely used in the United States until the 1850s, when it was replaced by the wet-collodion negative and albumen positive processes. The overwhelming majority of daguerreotypes that survive are portraits.

Salted Paper Processes

Photogenic Drawings. William Henry Fox Talbot invented the process of making "photogenic drawings" about 1834 and used a refinement of it to make his first camera images in 1835—though he did not announce his invention until 1839. To make photogenic drawing paper, Talbot treated writing paper with common salt (sodium chloride) and silver nitrate, which reacted to form light-sensitive silver chloride. During the exposure, which lasted up to half an hour in bright sunlight, the negative image appeared gradually, without needing to be developed chemically. When the image was sufficiently clear, Talbot stopped the process by immersing the paper in a bath of fixing agent. To produce a positive, the negative was oiled or waxed to make it translucent, placed in contact with another sheet of sensitized paper, and exposed to sunlight.

Since photogenic drawings were made without any gelatinous emulsion, the surfaces of the prints are matte, and the images appear to be slightly embedded in the surface fibers of the paper. Prints on photogenic drawing paper usually ranged in color, when they were first made, from reddish-brown to purple, though chemical impurities or variations in the process often yielded tones of blue, yellow, mauve, orange, or brown. Few of Talbot's prints retain their original color today, since Talbot did not fix and wash his prints adequately. Many of the prints in surviving copies of *The Pencil of Nature* have faded very badly (some almost to the point of total disappearance of the image), and most have changed in color from rich sepia or purple to rather unattractive shades of greenish-gray or yellowish-brown.

Calotype. The calotype process, which Talbot patented in 1841, was a refinement of the photogenic drawing process. Calotypes required much briefer exposures than did photogenic drawings, but they had to be developed after exposure to reveal the latent image. The calotype process was generally used only to make negatives, while the photogenic drawing process continued to be used for positives.

Calotype paper reduced exposure times to a few seconds. Although it would have been perfectly possible for Talbot to make prints as well as negatives on calotype paper, he preferred to use photogenic drawing paper for this purpose, since he felt that it yielded tints that were "more harmonious and pleasing to the eye." Prints on calotype paper were grayish brown. Most of the prints in *The Pencil of Nature*—including that of *The Haystack (see page 40)*—were made by printing calotype negatives on photogenic drawing paper.

Because paper negatives slightly diffused the light that passed through them in printing and produced an effect that was characterized as painterly, they were used most widely for such "artistic" subjects as still lifes, landscapes, genre scenes, and architectural studies. Except for the extraordinary body of work that David Octavius Hill and Robert Adamson made in Scotland during the 1840s, there are relatively few surviving portraits made with salted paper processes. Most patrons of portrait studios evidently preferred the greater illusion of realism offered by daguerreotypes.

Blanquart-Evrard's Calotype Process. The publication of *The Pencil of Nature*, which was issued in parts between 1844 and 1846, demonstrated the most important advantages of Talbot's paper processes over daguerreotypy—specifically, that the former could produce numerous prints from a single negative and that those prints could be mounted onto the pages of books. Talbot's practice of printing on photogenic drawing paper, however, made the printing operation too slow to be feasible for a commercial publisher producing large editions.

In France, where the daguerreotype reigned supreme during the 1840s, Louis-Désiré Blanquart-Evrard experimented with ways of speeding up the printing process and with methods of making prints that would be more permanent than Talbot's were. Blanquart-Evrard arrived at an improved form of calotype paper for his prints. Like the calotype paper that Talbot used for his negatives, this printing paper was (by the standards of the day) extremely sensitive to light and, after being exposed, had to be developed chemically to reveal the image. At his photographic printing and publishing house in Lille, which was in operation between 1851 and 1855, Blanquart-Evrard's production line could make over two hundred prints a day from each of ten or twenty negatives. Blanquart-Evrard usually had these prints mounted into books and albums. The prints, toned with gold chloride, had a rich reddish-brown or purplish-gray tone.

Blanquart-Evrard's technical improvements and publishing activities stimulated the brief but very great era of French salt prints. In the early 1850s, Edouard-Denis Baldus, Charles Nègre, Nadar, Victor Regnault, and the Bisson brothers were among the outstanding photographers who used salted paper processes. Although these processes were soon rendered obsolete by the wet-collodion and albumen processes, some photographers at first mixed the old and the new by making salt prints from collodion negatives or albumen prints from calotype negatives, while still others, including Blanquart-Evrard himself, sometimes applied a coat of albumen over their finished salt prints—just as a painter would varnish a completed canvas.

Albumen Print

Once the albumen positive and wet-collodion negative processes had been announced—in 1850 and 1851, respectively—it was inevitable that they would soon outdate both salt paper processes and daguerreotypy, for the combination of collodion negatives and albumen prints offered both the reproducibility of calotypes (which were slightly diffuse) and the clarity of daguerreotypes (which were unique positives).

Albumen printing paper was invented by Blanquart-Evrard in 1850, but he did not use it in his printing establishment, because it required much longer exposures than did his version of calotype paper. Despite this drawback, albumen was the predominant printing medium from the 1850s through the 1880s, when albumen paper was superseded by gelatin silver paper. Albumen paper was generally used to make prints from wet-collodion negatives.

By the mid-1850s, commercial producers coated one side of thin sheets of fine paper with a mixture of beaten egg white (albumen) and ammonium chloride or common salt (sodium chloride). The paper was sold in this form and could be stored for long periods of time. When the photographer was ready to use it, he had to sensitize it with a solution of silver nitrate (though, by the 1870s, presensitized paper was available commercially). The printing time could be reduced and tonal contrast increased if the paper was fumed with ammonia vapor before use.

The dried paper, which was not sensitive enough to use for making enlargements, was placed in contact with the negative in a printing frame and exposed for at least ten minutes—and sometimes for as long as an hour, depending on the available light. Like photogenic drawing paper, albumen paper "printed out" (i.e., produced a visible image during the printing, without having to be developed). After the exposure, the print was toned in a solution of gold chloride that changed the color of the print from an unattractive yellow to a rich reddish- or purplish-brown, depending on variations in processing. Because the paper used for albumen prints was usually thin and delicate, and because the albumen emulsion on one side gave the paper a tendency to curl, albumen prints were almost always mounted on cardboard.

Albumen prints are smooth and slightly glossy, with superb clarity of detail and extraordinarily subtle gradations of tones.

Albumen paper fell out of general use after the introduction of gelatin silver papers in the 1880s, but some photographers—including Atget—made albumen prints from dry-plate negatives as late as the 1920s.

Wet-Collodion Process

The wet-collodion process—a method of making negatives on glass plates—was perfected and published by the British sculptor and photographer Frederick Scott Archer in 1851. Within a few years it had totally supplanted the daguerreotype and salted paper processes.

In the first step of the wet-collodion process, a glass plate was evenly coated with a viscous solution of collodion and potassium salts. The plate was then sensitized by immersion in a bath of silver nitrate solution. The entire process of coating, sensitizing, exposing, and developing the plate had to be carried out within a matter of minutes—and much of it had to be done in the dark. It is, therefore, quite amazing that the wet-collodion process was so popular among explorer-photographers, such as W. H. Jackson and Timothy O'Sullivan, who had to travel with portable darkrooms. Some used tents made of light-proof cloth, while others outfitted wagons for the purpose. Explorer-photographers also had to contend with the great weight and fragility of glass plates, especially mammoth-sized ones. Large negatives were necessary if one wanted large prints, since the albumen paper that was usually employed to print wet-collodion negatives was sensitive enough only to make contact prints. This necessitated cameras large enough to handle huge plates—and these heavy cameras had to be mounted on tripods during exposures. The unprecedented clarity, tonal range, and reproducibility of wet plates offset the disadvantages of the process.

Bichromate Processes

Gum-Bichromate Print. W. H. Fox Talbot was so displeased with the impermanence of his salted paper prints that he began, about 1850, to experiment with methods of transferring photographic images to metal plates that could be etched and printed with ink—producing prints that would be as permanent as conventional etchings. In 1852, during the course of his experiments, he discovered that an emulsion of gelatin and potassium bichromate became very hard when exposed to light. (Chemists now refer to potassium *bi*chromate as potassium *di*chromate, but the earlier name—in its short form, "bichromate"—has remained in photographic usage.) This discovery eventually led to the invention of gum-bichromate prints, carbon prints, and woodburytypes—none of which uses either silver salts or printer's ink. It also led to the technique of photogravure, which is a refinement of Talbot's photo-etching process.

Bichromate printing was invented in 1855 by Alphonse Louis Poitevin, who realized that Talbot's discovery of the hardening of a gelatin-and-bichromate emulsion could be used in a direct method of printing rather than in an intermediary process in photo-etching. Poitevin simply added carbon black to the emulsion. The thickness of the emulsion on the finished print would determine the density of the pigment and would thereby register highlights and shadows. After 1890, when the process became popular, photographers usually substituted gum arabic for gelatin in the emulsion—and the process became known as gum bichromate.

To make a gum-bichromate print, the photographer first brushed onto a sheet of paper a mixture of gum arabic, bichromate, and pigment. Once the paper was dry, it was printed in contact with a negative. The greater the intensity of light that passed through a given area of the negative (and thus the darker the corresponding area of the print was to be), the deeper the hardening action extended into the emulsion. After the exposure, the print was soaked in water, which dissolved away most of the unhardened emulsion. The densest and thickest areas formed the shadows, while the thinnest areas—where the white paper backing was most visible through the translucent emulsion—formed the highlights.

The main problem with gum-bichromate prints was due to the fact that some light penetrated through all parts of the negative, causing a skin of hardened emulsion to form over the entire surface of the print. The soluble emulsion was underneath this skin. Since not all of the soluble emulsion could be washed away, and since the dissolving process left spaces between the hardened emulsion and the paper, the resulting print tended to be rather diffuse.

When the bichromate process was introduced in the mid-1850s, it did not become widely used, since photographers didn't like its lack of definition. Explorer-photographers, as well as their stay-at-home colleagues, wanted their pictures to be filled with precisely articulated facts—an effect best achieved with albumen prints. It was only around 1890, when photographers who thought of themselves as artists (i.e., the Pictorialists) reacted against this scientific attitude, that the "artistic" softness, imprecision, and coloration of the bichromate process became fashionable.

One of the reasons that the gum-bichromate process became so popular among the Pictorialists was that the prints looked somewhat like watercolors. The photographer could use in the emulsion a pigment of whatever color suited his fancy. He could also use any kind of artist's paper, making the prints seem more like drawings. Furthermore, while the surface of the print was wet, he could manipulate it with a paintbrush—eliminating details, changing tonal values, and making painterly brushmarks.

The gum-bichromate process was sometimes used in combination with other processes—as in the case of Steichen's photograph of the Flatiron Building *(see page 71),* in which he printed a gum-bichromate emulsion over a gelatin silver print from the same negative. By doing so, Steichen was able to combine the sharpness of detail and the tonal subtleties of the gelatin silver process with the painterly pigmentation and atmospheric softness of the gum bichromate.

Carbon Print. Although conventional bichromate prints were not sharp enough to suit the tastes that prevailed between the 1850s and the 1880s, the permanence of prints made with pigments and hardened bichromate emulsions was so much greater than that of prints made with silver halides that researchers continued their efforts to develop a form of bichromate printing that would yield sharply defined images.

A satisfactory process—carbon printing—was finally patented in England by Joseph Wilson Swan in 1864. Swan manufactured paper that was coated with an emulsion of gelatin, bichromate, and carbon black. This prepared paper, which was almost exactly like that used for conventional bichromate prints, was called "carbon tissue," even though it was quite thick. What distinguished Swan's process was that after the paper had been exposed, he adhered the hardened top surface of the carbon tissue (which had been in contact with the negative) to a fresh sheet of paper coated with clear gelatin. He then soaked this "sandwich" until he could pull the original paper backing of the carbon tissue away from the layer of emulsion that had remained soluble. With continued soaking, this soluble emulsion—which was now fully exposed to the water—could be thoroughly dissolved and washed away, leaving the relief pattern of the hardened emulsion on the surface of the print. As in a conventional bichromate print, the thickest parts of the emulsion formed the darkest shadows, while the thinnest parts formed the brightest highlights. Intermediate thicknesses produced a full range of grays.

Because all of the emulsion that hadn't been hardened by the action of light could be removed, and because the flat side of the hardened emulsion was against the paper support (rather than on the surface of the print, as in conventional bichromate prints), carbon prints provided very sharp definition. Although the carbon black that gave the process its name was the most commonly used pigment, any other pigment could be used. Carbon prints can thus be any color. The prints in Annan's book *(see pages 56 and 58)* are a rich brownish-black.

Woodburytype. Patented in England by Walter B. Woodbury in 1864, the woodburytype process used a hardened gelatin-and-bichromate emulsion, like that in carbon printing, to produce a lead mold from which many impressions of the image could be printed.

After the exposure with the negative, the resulting hardened gelatin relief was covered with a lead plate and placed in a hydraulic press that transferred the relief—in intaglio—into the lead. The lead mold was then placed in a hand press and filled with a solution of gelatin and pigment—but no bichromate, since the rest of the process was mechanical rather than photochemical. A sheet of paper was placed over the mold, and the image was printed by pressure. Since the margin of excess gelatin surrounded the image on the paper, the print had to be trimmed right at the edges of the image and mounted onto another sheet of paper.

Because several tons of pressure per square inch were required to make the lead molds, the presses of the second half of the nineteenth century, when woodburytypes flourished, could handle only relatively small images. Woodburytypes, like carbon prints, could be produced with pigment of any color. The woodburytypes in Thomson's book *Street Life in London (see page 64)* are a dark, rich purplish brown—quite similar in appearance to a gold-toned albumen print. Like gum-bichromate prints and carbon prints, woodburytypes are very resistant to fading or alterations of color.

Many connoisseurs consider woodburytypes to be the most beautiful of all photo-mechanically produced prints—especially since almost all other processes that use a printing press break up the image with grainy textures or patterns of tiny dots. Woodburytypes have no grain, and their tones are continuous.

Photogravure. Photogravure is essentially a cross between the technique of traditional aquatint and that of carbon printing. The process was invented in the late 1870s by Karl Klič, a Czech living in Vienna.

Klič began by preparing a copper plate exactly as if he were going to make an aquatint: he dusted it with powdered resin and then held the plate over a flame until the resin had melted sufficiently to adhere to the plate. This step produced an even and very fine grainy coating over the entire surface of the plate.

Klič then made a positive transparency—like a lantern slide—by printing onto a glass dry plate from the negative to be reproduced. This transparency was next contact-printed onto a sheet of paper coated with gelatin, bichromate, and pigment—just like that used in the first step of carbon printing. The exposed carbon tissue was then placed, gelatin side down, onto the prepared side of the copper plate. As in making a carbon print, the whole "sandwich" was soaked until the original paper backing could be removed and the soluble gelatin could be washed away. The plate was then etched and printed as if it were a conventional aquatint. The thinner the protective coating of gelatin, the more deeply the acid bit into the copper—and the darker the resulting areas in the finished print.

The soft, grainy tones of a photogravure are especially well suited to translating the tones of platinum and gum-bichromate prints into ink on fine paper. It is, therefore, not at all surprising that the Pictorialists, who favored those processes for their original prints, turned to photogravure for printed reproductions. In fact, most of the reproductions in Stieglitz's magazine *Camera Work* were very fine photogravures. In the deluxe edition of the magazine, they were usually printed on Japanese tissue paper and mounted onto heavier pieces of colored paper, which both gave a tint to the image through the very thin Japanese paper and provided a border, like a mat, all around the image. The heavy paper was, in turn, mounted onto the pages of the magazine. The photogravure of Stieglitz's photograph of the Flatiron Building *(see page 70)* was mounted on gray stock. For the special final issue of the magazine devoted to Strand's photographs—including that of the blind woman on page 80—Stieglitz felt that it was more in keeping with the power of the images to do away with the delicate tissue paper and to print the photogravures directly on heavy paper.

The Pictorialists liked photogravures not only for their tonal qualities but also for the connection that they established between photography and the traditional graphic arts—for they were engaged in a crusade to prove that photography could be a fine art. By presenting photographs as if they were aquatints, the Pictorialists hoped to demonstrate the legitimacy of their art.

Platinum Prints

The platinum process was invented in the 1870s by William Willis, an Englishman who, in 1879, established the Platinotype Company for the manufacture of platinum paper. Platinum prints, which are salted paper prints that substitute platinum salts for silver salts, do not have any glossy emulsion on their surfaces. The image, therefore, appears to be embedded in and upon the surface fibers of the paper. Platinum prints are matte and generally have a cool silvery- or bluish-gray tone, though early prints could be toned to a warm pinkish-tan, and later ones extended the range to yellowish-brown and greenish-gold. Platinum papers yielded much softer and subtler grays than did the gelatin silver papers that came on to the market at about the same time. The light values of platinum prints are concentrated toward the middle of the gray scale, without intense shadows or highlights. Platinum prints are, therefore, especially well suited to the romantic portraits, nudes, and landscapes that were much favored by the Pictorialists, who often overprinted platinum prints with gum bichromate.

Platinum paper was usually contact printed from gelatin dry plates. The image was formed by a series of chemical reactions that left a deposit of pure platinum—a very stable metal—on the paper. The denser the concentration of platinum in any given area, the darker that area appeared.

Platinum paper was available commercially from 1879 until about 1930, though from 1914 onward the inflated price of platinum made the paper very expensive. Throughout the period during which platinum paper was widely used, some photographers substituted palladium papers, which cost slightly less than platinum paper and gave very similar results.

One of the greatest exponents of platinum printing was Frederick H. Evans *(see page 74)*. During the early years of his career, Edward Weston *(see page 86)* also favored platinum prints. Edward Steichen experimented with the whole range of Pictorialist processes, including both platinum and palladium.

Gelatin Dry Plates and Gelatin Silver Film

The gelatin emulsion developed by Richard Leach Maddox in 1871 was improved by several experimenters before gelatin dry plates became commercially available around 1880. Dry plates—used to make negatives—were thin glass plates coated with an emulsion of gelatin in which light-sensitive silver bromide was suspended. The plates could be purchased ready to use and stored for long periods of time. They were so sensitive to light that they reduced exposure times to fractions of a second. And they could be developed long after being exposed. The amateur photographer could even send his exposed plates out to a commercial processing laboratory for developing and printing.

Because the gelatin silver printing papers that were perfected during the 1880s were so sensitive that they did not have to be placed in direct contact with the negative during printing—but could register images projected by strong artificial light through the negative and lenses—they made possible enlargements from small negatives. Dry plates could, then, be quite small and still produce large prints. The small plates led to small cameras, which were compact and light enough for the photographer to hold in his hands. Even if his hands were not perfectly steady, the exposures were so brief that slight movement would not blur the image. For the first time, it was possible to dispense with tripods and to record clearly the fleeting gestures of everyday life.

Dry plates for small cameras were superseded first by rolls of paper coated with an emulsion of gelatin and silver bromide and then, in 1889, by rolls of clear plastic film coated with the same emulsion. For several decades, however, glass dry plates continued to be used for large format cameras—which some photographers preferred to the small, hand-held ones because contact prints from large negatives offered greater clarity of detail than did enlargements from small negatives. Although dry plates were most frequently printed on gelatin silver paper, they could also be printed on platinum paper or with such Pictorialist processes as gum bichromate. As noted earlier, Atget continued into the 1920s to make albumen prints from glass dry plate negatives.

Because silver bromide is naturally sensitive only to the shortest wavelengths of light (toward the blue end of the spectrum), the earliest dry plates, like wet-collodion plates, tended to record blue as white and to record red, orange, and yellow as black. Orthochromatic film, whose emulsion contained a dye that extended the sensitivity of the silver bromide to orange and yellow—but not red—became common only in the 1890s. Panchromatic film, which contains additional dyes to enable it to distinguish reds, was developed around 1900 but

wasn't mass-produced until the 1930s. Even panchromatic film, however, records the values of colors toward the red end of the spectrum more darkly than they appear to the naked eye.

Like gelatin silver papers, gelatin silver films come in an astounding range of degrees of sensitivity ("speed"), graininess, and contrast. Combined with high-speed camera shutters and flashes, modern film can freeze virtually any movement at any point in its course. Furthermore, there are cameras and films available that can be used under practically any imaginable conditions. The choice of subject matter in photography can no longer be said to be limited by technology.

Gelatin Silver Prints

As its name implies, gelatin silver paper is coated with an emulsion of gelatin and silver salts—primarily silver bromide. This paper became commercially available in the 1880s, at about the same time at which gelatin dry plates became popular.

Gelatin silver papers are extremely versatile. They can have surface textures ranging from matte to glossy; they come in many degrees of sensitivity, graininess, and contrast; they can be used to make enlargements of virtually any size; and they can be toned to shades of brownish, yellowish, greenish, bluish, or purplish gray—though they are most commonly used to make standard black-and-white prints. Gelatin silver papers are almost always bought ready to use and are processed with commercially prepared developing and fixing solutions.

Gelatin silver papers must be developed after exposure to the negative in order to reveal the latent image. However, some early papers that used silver chloride instead of silver bromide printed out during the exposure. Silver bromide tends to give a cool cast to prints, while silver chloride gives warmer tones. Most modern papers, which increasingly substitute resin for gelatin, contain some silver chloride for warmth.

BIOGRAPHIES OF PHOTOGRAPHERS

Page numbers refer to reproductions of the photographer's work.

Abbott, Berenice   *pages 19, 125, 129, 133, 150, 152*

1898: Born in Springfield, Ohio. **1917–18:** Attended Ohio State University, Columbus. **1918–21:** Studied sculpture in New York. **1921:** Went to Paris to study sculpture with Antoine Bourdelle. **1923:** Began working as Man Ray's darkroom assistant. Learned photographic technique and processing from Man Ray. **1925:** In Man Ray's studio, first saw Atget's photographs. Learned that Atget lived nearby, went to visit him, and began buying prints from him. **1926:** Opened her own portrait studio, to which the Parisian intelligentsia flocked. Photographed Jean Cocteau, Marcel Duchamp, André Gide, James Joyce, Sylvia Beach, Peggy Guggenheim, and many others. **1928:** With the help of art dealer Julien Levy, acquired all the prints and negatives that had remained in Atget's studio at the time of his death in 1927. **1929:** Showed portraits in the Deutsche Werkbund exhibition *Film und Foto*, Stuttgart. Returned to New York, intending to stay for a brief visit. Decided to remain in New York and to make a thorough photographic documentation of the city. Supported herself with free-lance portraiture and photojournalism. **1935–39:** Continued documentation of New York under the auspices of the Federal Art Project of the Works Progress Administration. **1938–58:** Taught at the New School for Social Research, New York. **1939:** Published a selection of her New York photographs in her book *Changing New York*, with text by the art critic Elizabeth McCausland. **1949:** Illustrated with her photographs *Greenwich Village Today and Yesterday* by H. W. Lanier. **1950s:** Wrote several books about photographic technique. Photographed along U.S. Route 1. **1956:** Printed twenty Atget negatives for an edition of one hundred portfolios. **1958–61:** Made photographs to illustrate physical principles for physics textbooks. **1968:** Sold Atget collection to the Museum of Modern Art, New York. Moved to Maine. **1969–present:** Continues to photograph and to print her old negatives. Lives and works in Maine.

Adams, Ansel   *pages 61, 63, 118, 157*

1902: Born in San Francisco. **1914:** Began teaching himself to play the piano. **1916:** Went to Yosemite with his parents. Made his first photographs with a Brownie. Upon returning to San Francisco, began to study photography. **1917–19:** Photographed in Yosemite each summer. **1920:** Decided to become a professional concert pianist, but continued to photograph in Yosemite. **1927:** Published his first portfolio of photographs: *Parmelian Prints of the High Sierras*. First met Edward Weston. **1929:** Went to Santa Fe and Taos to work on book *Taos Pueblo* with writer Mary Austin. Met painters Georgia O'Keeffe and John Marin. **1930:** Returned to Taos. After meeting Paul Strand there and looking at his negatives, Adams decided to abandon his musical career and to become a professional photographer. *Taos Pueblo* published. **1932:** With Weston, Imogen Cunningham, Willard Van Dyke, and others founded Group f.64, devoted to promoting straight, sharp-focus photography, as opposed to the manipulated, soft-focus aesthetics of Pictorialism. The term "f.64" refers to the lens aperture setting that yields the sharpest focus over the entire area of the image. **1933:** Traveled to New York. Met Alfred Stieglitz. **1936:** First one-man show at Stieglitz's gallery, An American Place. **1937:** Moved to Yosemite. Went to the High Sierra with Weston. Traveled in the Southwest with David McAlpin and Georgia O'Keeffe. Included in Beaumont Newhall's Museum of Modern Art survey exhibition of the history of photography. **1939:** Went to New York. Met photographic historians Beaumont and Nancy Newhall. **1940:** Helped Newhall and McAlpin establish the photography department at the Museum of Modern Art in New York. **1941:** Photo-muralist for the U.S. Department of the Interior. Photographed in national parks. **1942:** Worked with Dorothea Lange for the Office of War Information. **1945–present:** Continues to photograph. Many lectures and workshops. Wrote series of basic photography manuals. Prints his earlier work. Lives and works in Carmel, California.

Alinari, Giuseppe, Leopoldo, and Romualdo (Fratelli Alinari) *page 52*

late 1820s–early 1830s: The brothers were born in Florence, Italy. **c. 1845:** Leopoldo was apprenticed to Giuseppe Bardi, an engraver who was interested in photography. **late 1840s:** Leopoldo learned photography from Bardi. **1852:** With Bardi's assistance, Leopoldo opened a photographic studio in Florence. **1854:** Giuseppe and Romualdo became partners in Leopoldo's business. They named the firm Fratelli Alinari, Fotografi Editori (Alinari Brothers, Photographic Publishers). **late 1850s:** Leopoldo photographed architecture and works of art all over Italy. Giuseppe and Romualdo managed the business. **early 1860s:** The brothers expanded their photographic publishing operations and opened a portrait studio. **1865:** Leopoldo died. **1865–71:** While Florence was the capital of the Kingdom of Italy, the photographers employed by Giuseppe and Romualdo made portraits of the political, cultural, and social elite, including King Vittorio Emanuele. **1870s:** The brothers began to employ photographers all over Italy to document art, architecture, and daily life. The firm's photographs were sold throughout Europe. **1880s–1920:** The firm continued to grow. After the deaths of Giuseppe and Romualdo, Leopoldo's son Vittorio became head of the business. **1920:** The firm was sold to a group of Florentine businessmen. **1920–present:** The firm has continued as a major publisher of photographs of art and architecture.

Alvarez Bravo, Manuel *page 117*

1902: Born in Mexico City. Both father and grandfather were painters who also photographed. **1908–14:** Attended Catholic Brothers' school in Tlalpan, near Mexico City. **1915:** Worked as a copy clerk. At night, studied accounting. **1916:** Began working as an office boy for the Mexican Treasury Department. **1917:** At night school, shifted from accounting to literature. **1918:** At night, studied painting and music at the Academia Nacional de Bellas Artes. **1922:** Worked for the Mexican Power and Transportation Department. Became interested in photography. Began to subscribe to photography magazines. **1924:** Bought his first camera. **1925:** Moved to Oaxaca to work for the Treasury Department. **1926–27:** Experimented with semi-abstract photographs of curved and folded paper. **1927:** Returned to Mexico City. Met Tina Modotti. Began his mature photographic work—images filled with the semi-surrealistic overtones of Mexican life. **1927–30:** Worked as a typist for the Treasury and Agriculture Departments. **1929:** Sent a portfolio of photographs to Edward Weston in the hope that he might include them in the Deutsche Werkbund exhibition *Film und Foto*, whose American section he was organizing. The portfolio reached Weston too late, but Weston responded with a letter of encouragement and praise. **1930:** When Tina Modotti was deported from Mexico, she gave Alvarez Bravo her eight by ten camera and a supply of platinum paper. Took over some of her jobs of photographing paintings. **1930–31:** Worked as a cameraman on the Russian director Sergei Eisen-

stein's film *Que Viva México*. **1931:** Began free-lance photography. Specialized in photographing works of art. Continued personal work. **1933:** Met Paul Strand. **1934:** Made film *Tehuantepec* about a workers' strike. Met Henri Cartier-Bresson. **1935:** Exhibited with Cartier-Bresson and Walker Evans at Julien Levy's gallery in New York. **1938:** Met the Surrealist writer André Breton, who was visiting Mexican muralist Diego Rivera. Became interested in Surrealist movement. **1930s–present:** Continued personal photographic work in addition to commercial photography and cinematography. Has taught photography in various schools in Mexico City. Lives and works in Mexico City.

Annan, Thomas *pages 56, 58*

1829: Born in Glasgow, Scotland. **late 1840s–early 1850s:** Worked as a copper-plate engraver. **1855:** Opened a calotype studio in Glasgow. Became especially known for his architectural studies, landscapes, and photographs of works of art. **c. 1860:** Began making naturally posed portraits without props. **1868:** Commissioned by the Glasgow City Improvement Trust to photograph Glasgow slums. **1873:** Annan's brother Robert became a partner in his studio. **1878:** Published *Photographs of Old Closes, Streets, &c., taken 1868–1877*, containing carbon prints of forty of his photographs. **late 1870s:** Annan's son, J. Craig Annan, who later became an important Pictorialist photographer much admired by Alfred Stieglitz, joined the family firm. **1883:** Went to Vienna to learn photogravure process from its inventor, Karl Klič. Introduced photogravure into Great Britain. **1887:** Died in Glasgow.

Atget, Eugène *pages 47, 55, 57, 65, 68, 75, 76, 79, 82, 108*

1857: Born in Libourne, near Bordeaux, France. **1870s:** After completing his secondary education, worked for several years as a cabin boy on a merchant ship. **c. 1880:** Studied acting at the National Conservatory of Dramatic Arts in Paris. After graduation, his acting career was limited to minor roles in repertory companies that toured the Parisian suburbs and the French provinces. What roles he was able to secure often came through the intervention of Valentine Delafosse, a modestly successful actress with whom Atget lived until her death in 1926. **1896:** Atget failed to obtain a renewal of his theatrical contract. **1897:** Tried his hand at painting but realized by the end of the year that he had no future as a painter. **1898:** At the age of forty-one, Atget turned to photography. After teaching himself the rudiments of his new art, he set out to photograph "everything in Paris and its environs that is artistic and picturesque." Began photographing street vendors and tradespeople. **1899–1914:** Made a methodical, street-by-street survey of the old quarters of Paris. Sold prints to such public institutions as the Bibliothèque Nationale, the Musée Carnavalet (the museum of the history of Paris), and the Musée des Arts Décoratifs in Paris and the Victoria and Albert Museum in London. Some of his photographs were published as book illustrations and on postcards. Also sold photographs to artists and designers for use as source material. **1914–18:** World War I forced him to give up photographing outdoors. Photographed interiors. **1920:** Sold to the Caisse National des Monuments Historiques a collection of two thousand five hundred negatives, which Atget described as "artistic documents of fine sixteenth-to nineteenth-century architecture in all the ancient streets of old Paris . . . historical and curious houses, fine facades and doors, panellings, door-knockers, old fountains, period stairs (wood and wrought iron), and interiors of all the churches in Paris (overall views and details)." **1920s:** Returned to many of the sites he had photographed earlier and made new images that sought to capture the mood rather than the details of his subjects. Photographed at Versailles. **1925:** Made a superb series of photographs of the neglected gardens of the Château de Sceaux in various seasons. Met the American photographer Berenice Abbott, who was to purchase and preserve his work after his death. **1927:** Died in Paris.

Baldus, Edouard-Denis   *page 44*

1813: Born in Paris. **1830s–early 1840s:** Studied painting. **1842:** First exhibited a painting in the Salon. **mid-1840s:** Lived for a few years in New York. **late 1840s:** Returned to France. Began photographing. **1849:** Photographed in the Midi of France. **1851:** Was the first photographer to be sent by the Commission des Monuments Historiques on an expedition to photograph architectural monuments throughout France. **1852:** Wrote a pamphlet whose title may be translated as "Photography competition, a memorandum put before the Secretary of the Society for the Encouragement of National Industry, with the assistance of whom the principal historic monuments of the Midi of France were reproduced by order of the Minister of the Interior by Edouard Baldus, painter." Published in Paris. **1852–57:** Photographed the progress of the construction work joining the Louvre and the Tuileries Palace. Also photographed other important buildings and monuments in Paris. **late 1852–early 1853:** Returned to the Midi to photograph. **1855:** Commissioned by Baron James de Rothschild to photograph the Chemin de Fer du Nord, one of the railroad lines of which he was a director. **1859:** Photographed the railroad line from Paris to the Mediterranean. **1870s:** Published many of his photographs and sold them in albums to tourists. **1882:** Died in Paris.

Baltz, Lewis   *pages 149, 168*

1945: Born in Newport Beach, California. **1967:** Began photographing cars and buildings. **1969:** Received B.F.A. degree from San Francisco Art Institute. **1969–71:** Studied art and architecture at Claremont Graduate School, Claremont, California. **1971:** Took a course in contemporary art—including Minimalism—at Claremont. Received M.F.A. degree. **early 1970s:** Began photographing tract houses. **1973–74:** Made the photographs for his book *The New Industrial Parks near Irvine, California.* Book published in United States and Germany. **1976:** Was one of twenty-four photographers commissioned by Joseph E. Seagram & Sons, Inc., to photograph American county courthouses as a part of the firm's Bicentennial Court House project. Was awarded a John Simon Guggenheim Memorial Fellowship. Commissioned by the Corcoran Gallery of Art, Washington, D.C., to photograph in Maryland. **1976–77:** Photographed housing developments in Nevada. **1978–79:** Made an extensive photographic documentation of the construction of a vacation-home development in Park City, Utah. **1980:** Published book *Park City.* Lives and works in Sausalito, California.

Beaton, Cecil   *page 123*

1904: Born in London. **1915:** Received his first camera and

began to photograph. **1917–22:** Attended Harrow School. Photographed on vacations. Style was influenced by the great fashion photographer Baron de Meyer. Made Pictorialist photographs with theatrical costumes and props. **1922–25:** Studied at St. John's College, Cambridge. Continued photography, especially portraits. **1925:** Worked briefly for family timber company. **1926:** Worked for a cement company. Tried unsuccessfully to sell his photographs for publication. Went to Venice, where he met Sergei Diaghilev, impresario of the Ballets Russes, who encouraged him in photography. Upon his return to London, opened a portrait studio in his family's house. At first, photographed mostly debutantes. **1927–29:** Increasing success as a portraitist. Became known for his "modernistic" style. **1929:** Traveled to New York, where he photographed socially prominent women. Showed his work to the editor of *Vogue,* who commissioned him to photograph for the magazine. **1930:** Signed contract to photograph in London exclusively for Condé Nast Publications, including *Vogue.* Returned to London. **1930s:** Became extremely fashionable portraitist. Portraits became quite surrealistic. Photographed fashions, parties, and ballet. Several trips to Hollywood to photograph movie stars. **1937:** Photographed the Duke and Duchess of Windsor in France. Traveled extensively in Europe. **1939:** Summoned to Buckingham Palace to photograph the queen. **1940:** Began photographing for the British Ministry of Information. Photographed war damage in London. **1941:** Photographed Royal Air Force operations in England. **1942:** Official photographer for RAF in Cairo. **1943–44:** Sent by Ministry of Information to India, Burma, and China. **1945–late 1970s:** Portraits of the rich and the famous. Published widely. Traveled extensively, especially to New York and Los Angeles. Designed sets and costumes for many ballets, plays, and films. Published many books of photographs and memoirs. **1972:** Knighted by Queen Elizabeth. **1980:** Died in Wiltshire, England.

Bisson, Louis-Auguste and Auguste-Rosalie (Bisson Frères)   *page 53*

1814: Louis-Auguste born in Paris. **1826:** Auguste-Rosalie born in Paris. **1830s:** Louis-Auguste worked as an architect. Auguste-Rosalie worked as an inspector of weights and measures at Rambouillet. **1841:** The brothers opened a daguerreotype portrait studio in Paris. **1848–49:** Made nine hundred daguerreotype portraits of members of the Assemblée Nationale. **c. 1850:** Stopped making daguerreotypes in favor of negative/positive processes. At first made salt prints, but as soon as wet-collodion negative and albumen positive processes were published (in 1851), began to use them. **1853:** Photographed Rembrandt etchings for Charles Blanc's *L'Oeuvre de Rembrandt,* the first book illustrated with photographs printed from glass-plate negatives and the first scholarly art book illustrated with photographs. **1855:** Magnificent architectural studies in France, Belgium, Germany, and Italy. Spectacular views of alpine scenery and glaciers. Much of this work was done on mammoth-sized wet-collodion plates (up to thirty by forty inches). The brothers' virtuosity in coating these huge plates without streaks or bubbles was unparalleled in France. **1860–62:** Auguste-Rosalie photographed expeditions climbing Mont Blanc. The brothers also photographed in Italy. **1864:** Forced out of business by the craze for small carte-de-visite photographs, which made their large views unfashionable. **1865–71:**

Worked for various photographic studios in Paris. **1876:** Louis-Auguste died in Paris. **1900:** Auguste-Rosalie died in Paris.

Bourke-White, Margaret

page 91

1904: Born in New York. **1921:** Studied photography with Clarence H. White at Columbia University. **1927:** Graduated from Cornell University. **1927-28:** Worked as a free-lance photographer in Cleveland. In local factories, made her first photographs of machinery. Some photographs published nationally. **1929:** Hired by Henry Luce as an associate editor and chief photographer of *Fortune,* the first issue of which appeared in February 1930. Specialized in photographs of industry and machinery. **early 1930s:** Worked six months each year for *Fortune,* the other six did free-lance advertising photography. **1930:** Made the first of three trips in consecutive years to photograph industry in the Soviet Union. **1936:** Traveled through the American South with writer Erskine Caldwell and photographed for their collaborative book *You Have Seen Their Faces*, a powerful study of rural poverty. Transferred by Henry Luce from *Fortune* to his new venture, *Life.* The cover of the first issue bore her photograph of Fort Peck Dam in Montana, and the lead story was her photo-essay on the men and women working on the government-sponsored dam project. **1937:** *You Have Seen Their Faces* published. **1938:** Worked with Erskine Caldwell on *North of the Danube*, a documentation of Czechoslovakia. **1941:** Was the only foreign photojournalist in Moscow when Germany bombed the city. **1941-45:** Extensive coverage for *Life* of the war in Europe and North Africa. Photographed the liberation of prisoners from German concentration camps at the end of the war. **1945-48:** Photographed in India. **1950:** Photographed in South Africa. **1952:** Covered the Korean War. Photographed New York and San Francisco from a helicopter. **c. 1956:** Parkinson's disease brought an end to her photographic career. **1971:** Died in Connecticut.

Bravo, Manuel Alvarez *see* Alvarez Bravo, Manuel

Brady, Mathew B.

page 46

c. 1823: Born near Lake George, New York. **c. 1840:** Learned daguerreotypy from Samuel F. B. Morse in New York City. **1844:** Opened daguerreotype portrait studio in New York. **1845:** Decided to try to photograph every illustrious American of his time. Among those whom he photographed during the following twenty years were John Quincy Adams, Daniel Webster, Henry Clay, Edgar Allan Poe, James Fenimore Cooper, Abraham Lincoln, and Robert E. Lee. **1858:** Opened a portrait studio in Washington, D.C. **1861:** When the Civil War broke out, Brady hired a corps of photographers to document the conflict. Although he published the photographs under his own name, most of them were actually made by such men as Alexander Gardner and Timothy O'Sullivan. Spent about $100,000 of his own money on the venture. **1865:** The public, wanting to forget the war, did not buy many of Brady's photographs, nor did the government reimburse him to the extent he had expected. Gradually became ruined financially. **1870s-early 1890s:** Small-scale portrait photographer in Washington, D.C. **1896:** Died in poverty in New York City.

Brandt, Bill

page 115

1904: Born in London. **1920s:** Educated in Germany. **c. 1927:** Recovered from tuberculosis in a sanatorium in Switzerland. **1928:** Photographed in the streets of London's East End. **1929:** Went to Paris to work as Man Ray's assistant. Influenced by the work of Man Ray, Kertész, Atget, and Brassaï. **1930:** Freelance photography for Parisian magazines. **1931:** Returned to London. **1930s:** Free-lance photography for many publications, including *The Weekly Illustrated, Lilliput,* and *Picture Post.* **1936:** Published book *The English at Home.* **1937:** Photographed poverty in industrial cities in northern England, including Newcastle. Photographed unemployed coal miners and their families. Photographs published widely. **1938:** Published book *A Night in London,* inspired by Brassaï's *Paris de Nuit.* **early 1940s:** Photographed London blacked out during the Blitz—empty streets, bomb damage, people sleeping in Underground stations and other shelters. **1945:** Began series of distorted, surrealistic nudes. Series continues to the present. **1940s-70s:** Many portraits of English and French writers and artists. Many of these portraits are quite surrealistic. Work extensively published and exhibited. Lives and works in London.

Brassaï

page 130

1899: Born Gyula Halász in Brassó, Transylvania (then part of Hungary, now in Rumania). **early 1920s:** Studied painting in Budapest and Berlin. **1924:** Moved to Paris. Adopted the pseudonym Brassaï, based on the name of his native town. Worked as a journalist. **1929:** Through his friend André Kertész, became interested in photography. Learned from Kertész how to photograph at night. Bought a six-and-a-half by nine-cm Voigtländer camera with a Heliar 4.5 lens. **1929-33:** Extensive photographic documentation of Paris at night. **1933:** Published his book *Paris de Nuit.* **1930s-50s:** Photographed many artists living in Paris. **1946:** Published a book of his drawings. **1955:** Made short film *Tant Qu'il y Aura des Bêtes (As Long as There Will Be Beasts).* **1960:** Published a book of photographs of graffiti. Lives and works in Paris.

Bruguière, Francis

page 128

1879: Born in San Francisco. **1890s:** Attended private schools and spent time in Europe, where he studied painting. **1905:** Met Alfred Stieglitz and members of his circle in New York. Became seriously interested in photography. **1906:** Opened a photographic studio in San Francisco. **1910:** Was included in the International Photo-Secession Exhibition, organized by Stieglitz for the Albright Art Gallery, Buffalo, New York. **c. 1912:** Began experimenting with multiple-exposure and semi-abstract photographs. **1918:** Moved to New York. Began photographing for *Harper's Bazaar, Vanity Fair,* and *Vogue.* Also photographed productions for the Theater Guild. **c. 1923-25:** Directed and photographed a surrealistic, multiple-exposure film entitled *The Way*, which was never completed. **1926:** Began concentrating on photographs of light and shadow patterns on complex, abstract arrangements of cut paper. May have experimented with this genre as early as 1921. **1928:** Moved to London. **1929:** Was included in the Deutsche Werkbund exhibition *Film und Foto*, Stuttgart. **1930-32:** Collaborated with writer Oswell Blakeston on film of moving cut-paper abstractions. Photographed English cathedrals. **1932:** Traveled to New York. Made photographs of skyscrapers as studies for film that was never made. **1933–37:** Collaborated with graphic designer E. McKnight Kauffer on photographic posters and advertisements. **1940:** Gave up photography and returned to painting. **1945:** Died in Middleton Cheney, England.

Cartier-Bresson, Henri
page 163

1908: Born in Chanteloup, Seine-et-Marne, France. **1927–28:** Studied painting with the cubist André Lhote. **1931:** Spent most of the year hunting in the Ivory Coast. Contracted black-water fever. Returned to France. During recuperation, became seriously interested in photography. Early influences included Atget, Kertész, and Martin Munkacsi. **1932:** Traveled and photographed in France, Spain, Belgium, and Germany. Developed his mature style almost immediately. **1933:** Traveled and photographed in Spain and Italy. Work exhibited at Julien Levy's gallery in New York. **1934:** Traveled to Mexico. Met Manuel Alvarez Bravo, with whom he and Walker Evans exhibited at Levy's gallery in 1935. **1935:** Spent much of the year in New York. Studied cinematography with Paul Strand. **1936:** Worked with director Jean Renoir on his film *Une Partie de Campagne* (*A Day in the Country*). **1937:** Made a documentary film about hospitals in civil-war-torn Spain. **1939:** Worked with Renoir on *La Règle du Jeu* (*The Rules of the Game*). **1940:** Drafted into Film and Photo Unit of French army. Captured by the Germans. **1943:** Escaped from prisoner-of-war camp and joined French Résistance. **1943–45:** Photographed French artists and worked for the underground. **1945:** Made a documentary film about the return of prisoners of war to France. **1946–47:** Traveled in the United States. Photographed many American writers. **1947:** Became a founding member of Magnum, a photographers' cooperative agency. **1948–50:** Photographed extensively in Asia. Covered Gandhi's funeral and Chinese Communist revolution. **1954:** Photographed extensively in the Soviet Union. **1958–59:** Photographed in China. **1960–73:** Many photojournalistic assignments all over the world. **1973:** Decided to reduce photographic work and to concentrate on drawing. Lives and works in Paris.

Cunningham, Imogen
pages 21, 88, 102

1883: Born in Portland, Oregon. **1901:** Saw photographs by the Pictorialist Gertrude Käsebier reproduced in *The Craftsman* magazine and became interested in photography. Bought her first camera. Took a correspondence course in photography. **1903–7:** Studied chemistry at the University of Washington, Seattle. **1907–9:** Worked in the Seattle portrait studio of Edward Curtis, who is best known for his documentation of American Indians. Made platinum prints from Curtis's negatives. **1909:** Was awarded a scholarship to study photographic chemistry at the Technische Hochschule, Dresden. While there, developed a method of substituting cheap lead salts for expensive platinum salts in making photographic paper. **1910:** On return trip from Germany to Seattle, stopped in New York and met Alfred Stieglitz and Gertrude Käsebier. Subscribed to *Camera Work*. Upon return to Seattle, opened a portrait studio. **1912:** One-woman exhibition of her photographs at the Brooklyn Museum of Arts and Sciences. **1915:** Married the etcher Roi Partridge. Made soft-focus nude studies of Partridge on Mount Rainier. First child born. **1917:** Twin sons born. Moved to San Francisco. **1920:** Moved to Oakland, where Partridge began teaching at Mills College. **1923:** Met

Edward Weston. **mid-1920s:** Made close-up studies of flowers. **1929:** Showed flower studies at Deutsche Werkbund exhibition *Film und Foto*, Stuttgart. **1930s–60s:** Many portraits of artists, writers, and photographers. **c. 1931:** Began to photograph movie stars for *Vanity Fair*. **1932:** With Ansel Adams, Edward Weston, and others, founded Group f.64 (*see Adams biography*). **1934:** Traveled to New York to do assignment for *Vanity Fair*. Divorced from Roi Partridge. **1947:** Moved to San Francisco. Began teaching at San Francisco Institute of Fine Arts (now San Francisco Art Institute). **1960:** Traveled to Europe. Photographed artists and photographers, including Man Ray and August Sander. **1973:** Was awarded a John Simon Guggenheim Memorial Fellowship to print her old negatives. **1975:** Began a series of portraits of nonagenarians. She was then ninety-two. **1976:** Died in San Francisco.

Delamotte, Philip Henry
page 50

1820: Born in London (?). **1840s:** Landscape painter. Taught drawing at King's College, London. Learned photography. Began making calotypes. **1851–54:** Photographed the reconstruction of the London Crystal Palace in Sydenham. Used the newly announced wet-collodion process to make his negatives. **1855:** *Photographic Views of the Progress of the Crystal Palace, Sydenham, taken during the Progress of the Works, by desire of the Directors* was published in two volumes illustrated with 160 albumen prints. Delamotte also published many views of the Crystal Palace in stereograph form. **1889:** Died in London.

Eisenstaedt, Alfred
page 95

1898: Born in Dirschau, West Prussia. **1906:** Family moved to Berlin. **c. 1913:** Became a serious amateur photographer. **1914–18:** Served in the German Army. **1918:** Wounded in the German attack on Dieppe, France. **1920s:** Worked as a button-and-belt salesman in Berlin. Photographed in all spare time. **1928:** Began to sell photographs to newspapers and magazines. **1929:** Quit job and became full-time, free-lance photographer. **1929–35:** Many photojournalistic assignments. Traveled throughout Europe and to Ethiopia. **1935:** Immigrated to the United States. Settled in New York. **1936:** Hired as one of the original staff photographers for *Life* magazine. **1936–present:** Photographed some two thousand assignments and ninety covers for *Life*. Has published several books of his photographs—particularly of his portraits of seemingly every famous person of the period. Numerous exhibitions of his work. Lives and works in New York.

Erwitt, Elliott
pages 99, 127, 159

1928: Born in Paris of Russian parents. **1929–38:** Family lived in Milan. **1938:** Family returned to Paris. **1939:** Family immigrated to the United States. Stayed in New York for one year. **1940:** Family moved to Los Angeles. **1942–46:** Attended Hollywood High School. **1947–48:** Took photography courses at Los Angeles Community College. Worked part time in a photographic processing laboratory. **1948:** Moved to New York. **1948–51:** Free-lance photojournalism and portraiture. Worked on documentary projects for Roy Stryker (former head of RA and FSA photographic sections) at Standard Oil of New Jersey. **1951–52:** Drafted into the United States Army. Served with the Signal Corps in France. Met the great war photographer Robert Capa, who offered him membership in Magnum, the photographers' cooperative agency. **1950s–present:** Extensive photojournalism, advertising photography, and personal work. Has also made films. Lives and works in New York.

Evans, Frederick H. *page 74*

1853: Born in England. **early 1880s:** Began photographing and opened a bookstore in London. **1887:** Received a medal from the Royal Photographic Society for his photographs of natural forms taken through a microscope. **1889:** Met Aubrey Beardsley, who was a frequent customer in his bookstore. **c. 1890:** Began his extensive series of photographs of English and French medieval cathedrals. **1898:** Retired from his bookstore. **1900:** One-man exhibition at the Royal Photographic Society in London. Elected to the Fellowship of the Linked Ring, an important organization dedicated to photography as an art form. The Linked Ring was the British counterpart of Stieglitz's Photo-Secession in the United States. **1903:** Stieglitz devoted a special issue of *Camera Work* to Evans's work. George Bernard Shaw contributed an appreciation. **1905:** Began photographing on assignment for *Country Life* magazine. **1906:** Photographed French châteaux for *Country Life.* **1907:** Photographed in France. **1908–33:** Continued to photograph and to exhibit his work. **1943:** Died in London.

Evans, Walker *pages 73, 105, 109, 113, 124, 132, 135, 136, 138, 144, 146, 148, 166*

1903: Born in St. Louis, Missouri. **1903–25:** Raised in Kenilworth, Illinois (a suburb of Chicago) and in New York City. Attended the Loomis School and Phillips Academy, Andover, Massachusetts. Attended Williams College for one year. **1926:** Went to Paris. Studied at the Sorbonne. **1927:** Returned to New York. **1928:** Bought a camera that took two-and-a-quarter- by four-and-a-quarter-inch negatives and made his first serious photographs. **1929:** Bought his first 35mm camera. Began using a five- by seven-inch view camera. **1930:** Three of his photographs of Brooklyn Bridge published in the Black Sun Press edition of Hart Crane's poem *The Bridge.* Began using six- by eight-inch view camera. **1931–33:** Shared a studio with Ben Shahn in Greenwich Village, New York City. **1932:** Went to Cuba to make photographs to illustrate Carleton Beals's *The Crime of Cuba.* **1933:** Exhibition of his photographs of nineteenth-century American houses at the Museum of Modern Art. (The photographs were mostly made in New York City, New York State, and Connecticut.) Began to use an eight- by ten-inch view camera. **1935:** June–July: hired by the Resettlement Administration to photograph in West Virginia and Pennsylvania. December: Hired on a more permanent basis by the Historical Section of the Resettlement Administration. Photographed in Louisiana and Alabama. In addition to RA work, photographed antebellum architecture for himself. **1936:** January–February: Continued to photograph in Louisiana and Alabama. March: Photographed soil erosion in rural Mississippi and made extensive photo-documentation of Vicksburg. Then photographed in Georgia and South Carolina. Summer: Took a leave of absence from the RA to work on a project for *Fortune* magazine with his friend the writer James Agee. For two months, Evans and Agee lived with and recorded the lives of three sharecropper families in Hale County, Alabama. Evans also photographed in nearby towns, including Moundville. Agee's text and Evans's photographs were rejected by *Fortune,* but were eventually published (in 1941) as the book

Let Us Now Praise Famous Men. Evans's negatives went into the RA files. **1937:** Photographed flood refugees in Arkansas and Tennessee. Dismissed from RA when it became the Farm Security Administration. **1938:** Photographed Sixty-first Street between First and Third avenues in New York City for FSA. Published *American Photographs,* which accompanied a show at the Museum of Modern Art. Began making candid-camera portraits of New York City subway riders. **1943–45:** Writer for *Time* magazine. **1945–65:** On staff of *Fortune* magazine. Many photo-essays (in black and white and color) with his own texts. **1965–75:** Taught at Yale until his death in 1975.

Feininger, Andreas *page 151*

1906: Born in Paris. Son of artist Lyonel Feininger. **1922–25:** Attended the Bauhaus in Weimar, Germany. Specialized in cabinetmaking. **1925–28:** Studied architecture in Weimar and Zerbst, Germany. Became interested in photography. **1929–31:** Worked as an architect and photojournalist in Dessau and Hamburg. **1932–33:** Worked for Le Corbusier in Paris. Continued to photograph. **1933:** Moved to Stockholm. **1936–39:** Worked as an architectural photographer. Published a book of his photographs of Stockholm. **1939:** Moved to New York. **1940:** Worked as a photojournalist for the Black Star Agency. Did first assignments for *Life.* Began photographing New York. **1941:** Resigned from Black Star. Free-lance work, primarily for *Life.* **1943–62:** Staff photographer for *Life.* Photographed over three hundred stories for the magazine. **late 1940s–early 1950s:** Began series of photographs of bones, trees, and shells, with strong emphasis on overall pattern. **1950s:** Many photographs of sculpture. **1960s–70s:** Extensive travel in United States and Europe. Wrote many books on photographic technique. Continued series of photographs begun earlier. Lives and works in New York and Connecticut.

Frank, Robert *pages 155, 158, 164*

1924: Born in Zurich, Switzerland. **1942:** Began photographing seriously. **1943–44:** Worked as a cinematographer in Zurich. **1946:** Began to photograph in the streets of Zurich. **1947:** Immigrated to the United States. Commissioned by Alexey Brodovitch, art director of *Harper's Bazaar,* to photograph fashions. **1948–55:** Free-lance photography for *Harper's Bazaar, Fortune, Life, Look, The New York Times,* and other publications. Assignments in North and South America and in Europe. **1955:** Became first European-born photographer to be awarded a John Simon Guggenheim Memorial Fellowship. **1955–56:** Traveled all over the United States and photographed extensively, concentrating on the most characteristic and banal aspects of American life—people riding in cars, eating at lunch counters, listening to jukeboxes, etc. **1958:** His book *Les Américains* published in France. Began making films. **1959:** *The Americans* published in the United States. **1966:** Gave up still photography in favor of filmmaking. Lives and works in Nova Scotia, Canada.

Freund, Gisèle *page 131*

1913: Born in Berlin. **1928:** Received her first camera (a 35 mm Leica) as a gift from her father. Soon became an enthusiastic amateur photographer. **c. 1931–33:** Studied at the Institute for Social Research, Frankfurt. **1933:** Active in anti-Nazi student groups. Forced to flee to Paris. Entered doctoral program at the Sorbonne and began to write thesis on the sociology of nineteenth-century French photography. To support herself, began working as a photojournalist. **1936:** Her thesis was published by Adrienne Monnier, proprietor of the bookstore La Maison des Amis des Livres. Her photo-essay on unemployment in England was published in the newly founded *Life* magazine. **1938:** When 35 mm color film appeared on the market in France, Freund decided to make a series of color portraits of the great French and English writers. Adrienne Monnier gave her letters of introduction to such people as André Gide, Colette, Jean Cocteau, Jean-Paul Sartre, Simone de Beauvoir, James Joyce, Virginia Woolf, and T. S. Eliot. **1938–40:** Continued to do free-lance work for *Life*. **1940:** Forced by German invasion of France to flee. Invited to Argentina by writer and editor Victoria Ocampo. **1940s:** Free-lance photography throughout Latin America for American, British, and Latin American magazines. **1947–54:** Member of photographers' cooperative agency Magnum. **1954:** Photo-essay on Evita Peron for *Life* created an international diplomatic incident. **1950s–present:** Free-lance photographer, journalist, and historian of photography. Lives and works in Paris.

Friedlander, Lee   *page 21*

1934: Born in Aberdeen, Washington. **1948:** Began photographing. **late 1950s:** Photographed jazz musicians for record covers. **c. 1962:** Began photographing store windows, many with reflections, including that of the photographer. Also made series of photographs of switched-on television sets in hotel rooms. **1960s:** Traveled on free-lance magazine assignments all over the United States. Did personal work concurrently. **1967:** Photographs exhibited at the Museum of Modern Art in New York with work by Diane Arbus and Garry Winogrand. **1968:** While in New Orleans, discovered the negatives of the portraits of prostitutes that E. J. Bellocq had made around 1912 in the Storyville district of the city. Acquired the glass plates and printed them. **1968–71:** Series of photographs of parties. **1969:** Published portfolio of his own photographs and Jim Dine's etchings: *Work from the Same House*. **1970s:** Extensive series of photographs of trees, bushes, flowers, birds, and American monuments. **1975–76:** Photographed sculpture in the Hirshhorn Museum Sculpture Garden, Washington, D.C. Lives and works in New City, New York.

Hawes, Josiah Johnson *see* Southworth, Albert Sands and Josiah Johnson Hawes

Hine, Lewis W.   *page 90*

1874: Born in Oshkosh, Wisconsin. **1892:** Father died. Began working at various menial jobs to help support family. Independently studied drawing. **1898–1901:** Studied at the University of Chicago. **1901:** Began teaching science at the Ethical Culture School in New York. Attended School of Education, New York University. **c. 1903:** Began making photographs for use in teaching. **1904:** Began photographing immigrants on Ellis Island. Was assisted in project by Frank A. Manny, principal of Ethical Culture School. **1905:** Established extracurricular photography course at Ethical Culture School. **1906:** Began to publish articles about photography as an educational aid. Began free-lance photography for National Child Labor

Committee. **1907:** Photographed immigrants doing piecework at home in tenements, Lower East Side, New York. Enrolled in Columbia University graduate school to study sociology. Continued to teach at Ethical Culture School. Took photography class—including Paul Strand—to Stieglitz's "291" gallery. Began photographing for the Pittsburgh Survey, a documentation of urban industry and life. **1908:** Resigned from Ethical Culture School. For NCLC, photographed children working in factories and mines in Indiana, Ohio, West Virginia, and North Carolina. Photographs widely published. **1909:** Photographed for NCLC along the East Coast from Georgia to New England. Became staff photographer for *The Survey*, a magazine devoted to social and labor reform. **1910–18:** Extensive work all over the United States for NCLC. **1918:** Resigned from NCLC. Joined the American Red Cross. **1918–19:** Photographed for the ARC in France, Belgium, Italy, Greece, and the Balkans. **1920:** Began extensive series of portraits of working people performing their jobs. **1920s:** Many work portraits published in *The Survey* and other periodicals. **1930:** Began photographing construction of the Empire State Building. **1931:** Photographed for ARC in Kentucky and Arkansas. **1932:** Published *Men at Work*, a book of work portraits, including many Empire State photographs. **1933:** Made portfolio of photographs of mill workers: *Through the Loom*. Photographed dam projects for the Tennessee Valley Authority. **1935:** Applied for job with the Resettlement Administration but was rejected. **late 1930s:** Very few assignments. Frustration and poverty. **1940:** Died in Hastings-on-Hudson, New York.

Jackson, William Henry   *page 60*

1843: Born in Keesville, New York. **1844:** Family moved to Georgia. **1853:** Family moved to Troy, New York. Began to draw. **1857–61:** Worked in photographic portrait studios in Troy and in Vermont. **1862:** Enlisted in United States Army. Sketched army life. **1863:** Discharged from army. Worked in a photographic studio in Rutland, Vermont. **1866:** Traveled to New York and then across the country to Los Angeles. **1867:** Herded horses from Los Angeles to Wyoming. Continued east to Omaha, Nebraska. Opened a photographic studio in Omaha. **1868:** His brother became a partner in the studio. Did first photography for Union Pacific Railroad. Photographed Indians near Omaha. **1869:** Photographed in Wyoming. Received commission for ten thousand views of western landscape from publisher of stereographic views. **1870–78:** Official photographer for F. V. Hayden's surveys of the West, summers. Rest of the year in Omaha. **1870:** Photographed for survey from the Black Hills of Wyoming to Pike's Peak. **1871:** Photographed for survey in Yellowstone. **1872:** Largely as a result of Jackson's photographs, Congress declared Yellowstone the first national park. Returned with survey to Yellowstone. **1873:** Photographed for the survey in the Rocky Mountains, including Mountain of the Holy Cross. **1874:** Photographed for the survey in southwestern Colorado. **1875:** Photographed for the survey in southwestern Colorado and northwestern Arizona, including Canyon de Chelly. Began using twenty- by twenty-four-inch mammoth-plate camera. **1876:** Jackson's survey photographs shown at the Centennial Exposition in Philadelphia. Jackson attended daily to answer questions. **1877:** Photographed for the survey in New Mexico and Arizona. **1878:** Photographed in the Tetons and Yellowstone. End of the Hayden surveys. **1879:** Opened a photographic studio in Denver. **1881–94:** Made many photographs along western rail routes. Traveled and photographed extensively in the western United States and in Mexico. His photographs were widely distributed. **1894–95:** Traveled to New York and then on to London, Paris, Marseilles, Tunis, Tangiers, Cairo, and Bombay. Photographed extensively in India and Ceylon. Then traveled to Australia, New Zealand, Singapore, China, Japan, and Korea. **1896:** Traveled from Vladivostok to Moscow. Returned to New York. Many photographs from trip had been published over the course of the two years in *Harper's Weekly.* **1900–37:** Continued to make and to publish photographs. **1938:** Technical adviser for movie *Gone With the Wind.* **1940:** Published his autobiography, *Time Exposure.* **1942:** Included in exhibition *Photographs of the Civil War and the American Frontier* at the Museum of Modern Art in New York. Died in New York.

Kertész, André *pages 19, 49, 77, 84, 114, 116, 162, 167*

1894: Born in Budapest, Hungary. **1912:** Graduated from Academy of Commerce, Budapest. Worked as a clerk on the Budapest Stock Exchange. Bought first camera and began photographing street and genre scenes. **1914–18:** Served in the Austro-Hungarian Army during World War I. Photographed army life. **1919–24:** Photographed extensively in Hungary. **1925:** Moved to Paris. Soon became successful photojournalist, doing free-lance reportage for French, English, German, and Italian publications. Began photographing Parisian street life. Began making portraits of artists. **1928:** Bought his first Leica 35mm camera. **1933:** Series of nudes distorted in funhouse mirrors. **1936:** Arrived in New York. Planned to work for American magazines for a year or two, then return to Paris, but remained permanently in New York. **1937–49:** Did free-lance work for magazines, but instead of the reportage he wanted to do, ended up doing mostly fashion photography for *Harper's Bazaar* and *Vogue.* **1949–62:** Under contract with Condé Nast Publications to photograph interiors for *House and Garden.* **1963–present:** Devotes himself to his own photographic work. Lives in New York.

Lange, Dorothea *pages 67, 141, 143, 145, 154*

1895: Born in Hoboken, New Jersey. **1914–16:** Attended New York Training School for Teachers. **c. 1915:** Began working nights and weekends as an assistant in the studio of Arnold Genthe, a prominent portrait photographer. **1917:** Took a basic photography course taught by Clarence H. White at Columbia University. **1918:** Traveled to San Francisco and decided to remain there. Got a job in a photographic processing laboratory. **1919:** Opened a portrait studio. **1920:** Married Maynard Dixon, a painter of western wilderness life. **1921–33:** Successful portraitist. **1933:** Made her first documentary photograph—of a breadline near her studio. **1934:** Willard Van Dyke, a photographer and friend of Lange's, exhibited her documentary work in his gallery in San Francisco. Exhibition seen by Paul Taylor, a professor of economics at the University of California, Berkeley. **1935:** Hired by Taylor to photograph for the California State Emergency Relief Administration, of which he was the field director. With Taylor, prepared illustrated report on camps for migratory agricultural workers. Hired by Roy Stryker to photograph for the Historical Section of the Resettlement Administration. Divorced from Maynard Dixon. Married Paul Taylor. **1935–37:** Photographed extensively in California and the Southwest for the RA. **1937:** Reduced to

part-time work when RA became Farm Security Administration. **1938:** Traveled with Taylor throughout the West and the South to photograph and to gather material for their book, *An American Exodus,* which was published the following year. **1941:** Was awarded a John Simon Guggenheim Memorial Fellowship to photograph "the American social scene." Abandoned project after outbreak of the war. **1942:** Photographed interned Japanese-Americans for War Relocation Authority. **1945–50:** Illness prevented photographic work. **1951–63:** Many photojournalistic assignments and frequent travel all over the world. **1966:** Died in San Francisco.

Laughlin, Clarence John *page 160*

1905: Born at Lake Charles, Louisiana. **1910:** Family moved to New Orleans. **1918:** Father died. Left school to support mother and sister. **1924–35:** Various jobs, including bank clerk. **c. 1925:** Became interested in French poetry, especially Baudelaire and the Symbolists. Began writing poetry and Gothic fiction. **1934:** Began photography. Among early influences were Atget, Man Ray, Stieglitz, Strand, and Weston. **1936–40:** Photographed construction work along the Mississippi River for the United States Army Corps of Engineers. **1940:** Two-man show (with Atget) at Julien Levy's gallery in New York. **1940–41:** Fashion photography for *Vogue.* **1941–42:** Worked with Photography Department, National Archives, Washington, D.C. **1942:** Enlisted in United States Army. Worked as a photographer for Signal Corps and Office of Strategic Services. **1946:** Discharged from army. Returned to New Orleans. **1949–69:** Worked as architectural photographer. **1930s–present:** Surrealistic and symbolic photographs widely exhibited and published. Has written and lectured extensively on photography. Lives and works in New Orleans.

Lee, Russell *page 139*

1903: Born in Ottawa, Illinois. **1917–21:** Attended Culver Military Academy. **1921–25:** Attended Lehigh University, Bethlehem, Pennsylvania. Studied chemical engineering. **1925–28:** Worked for Certainteed Products Company of Marseilles, Indiana. Made composition roofing. **1928:** Moved to Kansas City to manage a Certainteed Products plant. **1929:** Quit job. Began painting. Moved to San Francisco. Lived on small independent income. **1931–36:** Lived in New York. Studied at the Art Students League under John Sloan. Summers in Woodstock, New York. **1933:** Traveled in Europe. **1935:** Bought his first camera, a 35mm Contax. Began photographing street life in New York. Began to sell photographs for publication. **1936:** Applied for photographer's job with Resettlement Administration. Given temporary assignment of photographing New Jersey Homesteads housing project. When Carl Mydans left RA, Lee was given his position. Photographed farmers in Iowa, Indiana, and Illinois. **1936–37:** Covered aftermath of flooding in Ohio and upper Mississippi valleys. Began using three-and-a-quarter by four-and-a-quarter format press camera with flash for interior work. Did a photo-essay on the daily life of a hired man on a typical Indiana farm. **1937:** Photographed for RA in Michigan, Wisconsin, and Minnesota. Spent several months in Washington, D.C. Was one of only two photographers (Arthur Rothstein was the other) retained on a full-time basis when RA became Farm Security Administration. **1937–42:** Extensive photography for FSA all over western half of United States. **1942:** Photographic section of FSA transferred to Office of War Information. Lee continued through the year. **1943-45:** Photographed for the Air Transport Command from the air over South America, the south Atlantic, Africa, Middle East, and Far East. Photographed extensively in China in 1944. **1946:** Photographed coal miners and their families in West Virginia and Kentucky for the U.S. Department of the Interior. **1947:** Hired by Roy Stryker (former head of RA and FSA photographic section) to photograph for Standard Oil of New Jersey. **1948-50:** Photographs appeared regularly in SONJ's magazine *The Lamp*. **1950-present:** Free-lance industrial photography. Also documentary photography in Texas and in Italy. Has taught extensively. Lives and works in Texas.

Man Ray
pages 87, 103

1890: Born Emmanuel Radensky (?) in Philadelphia. **1897:** Family moved to New York. **1908-12:** Attended Academy of Fine Arts and Ferrer School, New York. Began working as a typographer and graphic designer. **1910:** Met Alfred Stieglitz at his "291" gallery. **1915:** Exhibited his paintings at Charles Daniel's avant-garde gallery in New York. Met Marcel Duchamp. Began making collages and assemblages. **1918:** Bought a camera to make photographs of his paintings. Soon began experimenting with photography. **1921:** Moved to Paris. Supported himself by photographing artists and their works. Accidentally invented the Rayograph process by placing objects on photographic paper and exposing them to light (actually a variation of Fox Talbot's photogenic drawings). **1920s:** Made a wide range of photographic work, especially Rayographs and solarized nudes and portraits—in addition to his work in painting, sculpture, film, and other media. **1925:** Discovered Atget and showed his work to Berenice Abbott, who was then Man Ray's darkroom assistant. **1929:** Showed Rayographs in Deutsche Werkbund exhibition *Film und Foto*, Stuttgart. **1931:** Began photographing flowers close up. **1940:** Returned to the United States. Lived in Hollywood. Worked as fashion photographer and teacher. **1951:** Returned to Paris, where he continued his work in all media. **1976:** Died in Paris.

Marville, Charles
page 54

1816: Born in Paris. **1840s:** Worked as a painter, lithographer, and illustrator. **c. 1850:** Learned photography. **1851-55:** Photographs of architecture, sculpture, and landscapes appeared in various albums published by Louis-Désiré Blanquart-Evrard. **1852-70:** Photographed the old streets, the major architectural monuments, and the new parks of Paris for Baron Georges Haussmann, Prefect of the Seine. **1853:** Photographed landscapes and castles along the Rhine. **1850s-60s:** Official photographer of works of art for the Louvre. **1878 or 1879:** Died in Paris.

Model, Lisette
pages 81, 97

1906: Born Elise Seybert in Vienna. **1918-21:** Studied music with composer Arnold Schönberg. **1922:** Moved to Paris. **1922-36:** Continued to study music and voice. **1936:** Married painter Evsa Model. **1937:** Took up photography—both image-making and processing—as means of earning a living. Photographed in Paris and Nice. **1938:** Traveled to New York. Decided to remain. **1940:** In the course of applying for a laboratory technician's job at the newspaper *PM*, showed her portfolio to picture editor Ralph Steiner, who offered to publish seven photographs from the Promenade des Anglais series, made in Nice in 1937. Steiner showed Model's photographs to Alexey Brodovitch, the art director of *Harper's Bazaar*, who offered her free-lance work. Began to photograph in the streets and bars of New York's Lower East Side. **1941:** Photographs exhibited in a group show at the Museum of Modern Art. Photographs published in *PM* and *Harper's Bazaar*. **1941-51:** Free-lance photography for *Harper's Bazaar* and other periodicals. **1951:** Began teaching at the New School for Social Research, New York. **1953:** Traveled and photographed in Europe. **1954:** Photographed in Venezuela. **1954-64:** Intensive teaching. Students included Diane Arbus. **1965:** Was awarded John Simon Guggenheim Memorial Fellowship. **1966:** Traveled and photographed in Europe. **1967-present:** Numerous exhibitions and publications. Continues teaching. Lives and works in New York.

Modotti, Tina
pages 89, 93

1896: Born in Udine, Italy. **c. 1910:** Her father immigrated to United States. Settled in San Francisco. **1913:** Joined her father in San Francisco. Began working in a textile factory. **c. 1915:** Rest of the family arrived in San Francisco. **1917:** Married the poet and painter Roubaix de L'Abrie Richéy. Worked as a dressmaker. **1920-21:** Acted in several Hollywood films. Typecast as a passionate, jealous Italian woman. **1921:** Met Edward Weston. Her husband went for extended stay in Mexico City. Began affair with Weston. Became his favorite model. **1922:** Husband died of smallpox in Mexico City. Went to Mexico City for funeral. Showed Weston's photographs to Mexican artists and intellectuals. Found congenial artistic climate. Returned to San Francisco. Continued affair with Weston. **1923:** Moved with Weston to Mexico City. Learned photography from Weston. Made many friends among artists, intellectuals, and revolutionaries. **mid-1920s:** Extensive photographic work. Became involved in politics. **1926:** Affair with Weston ended. Weston returned to San Francisco. **1927:** Became a member of the Mexican Communist party. Exchanged work with Weston by mail. Her personal photography became socially and politically oriented. **1927-30:** Worked as a professional photographer specializing in reproductions of paintings. **1928:** Photographed murals by Diego Rivera, José Clemente Orozco, and others. Met the young Cuban revolutionary Julio Antonio Mella, who was studying law at the National University in Mexico City and working as a journalist. Began affair with Mella. **1929:** Was with Mella when he was assassinated. Was accused of complicity in his murder. Was found innocent. **1930:** Was accused of complicity in attempt to assassinate the President of Mexico, Pascual Ortiz Rubio. Was deported from Mexico. Went to Germany. Contened photography. Went to Moscow to live. **1931:** Abandoned photography. Began working for Soviet International Red Aid. **1936-39:** Worked for the Communists in Spain during the civil war. **1939:** Returned to Mexico under an assumed name. Worked as a translator. **1942:** Died in Mexico City.

Moholy-Nagy, László
pages 51, 69, 96, 98, 107

1895: Born in Bácbarsòd, in southern Hungary. **1913:** Began to study law at the University of Budapest. **1914:** At the outbreak of World War I, became an artillery officer in the Austro-Hungarian Army. **1917:** Severely wounded. In hospital, began making drawings and watercolors. **1918:** Resumed his study of law, but soon discontinued it. **1920:** Moved to Berlin. Became a member of the artistic avant-garde. **1922:** In collaboration with his wife, Lucia, began making photograms—semi-abstract images produced by placing small objects directly onto sheets of photographic paper and exposing them to light. **1923:** Joined faculty of the Bauhaus in Weimar. **c. 1925:** Began camera photography. **1925:** Traveled to France. Published *Painting Photography Film,* a book that was crucial in disseminating the new Constructivist photographic aesthetic of unexpected viewpoints, semi-abstract compositions, close-up portraits, and industrial and sociological subjects. The Bauhaus moved to Dessau. **1928:** Resigned from the Bauhaus. Moved to Berlin. **1929:** Traveled to Marseilles. Made the film *Marseille Vieux Port.* Exhibited ninety-seven of his photographs and photograms at the Deutsche Werkbund exhibition *Film und Foto* in Stuttgart, which he helped to organize. **1934:** Moved to Amsterdam, where he worked in commercial photography and design. **1935:** Moved to London, where he worked in graphic and commercial design. **1935–36:** Photographed extensively in London, Eton, and Oxford. **1936:** His photographs illustrated *The Street Markets of London* by Mary Benedetta. **1937:** His photographs illustrated *Eton Portrait* by Bernard Fergusson. Moved to Chicago. Appointed director of the New Bauhaus/American School of Design. School closed at the end of one year. **1939:** His photographs (along with many by others) illustrated *An Oxford University Chest* by John Betjeman. Founded The School of Design (later The Institute of Design) in Chicago. Graduates include many important photographers. **1946:** Died in Chicago.

Mudford, Grant

page 169

1944: Born in Sydney, Australia. **1963–64:** Studied architecture at the University of New South Wales, Sydney. **1965:** Opened a photographic studio in Sydney. **1965–71:** Did fashion, advertising, editorial, and theatrical photography. Also worked as a cinematographer on many short films. **1971–72:** Began concentrating on personal photography. **1974:** Received a Visual Arts Board Travel Grant from the Australia Council for the Arts. **1974–76:** Traveled and photographed in the United States. Began to photograph American industrial structures. **1977:** Received a second travel grant. Moved to Los Angeles. **mid-1970s–present:** Lives and works in Los Angeles.

Muybridge, Eadweard

pages 31, 32, 33

1830: Born Edward Muggeridge in Kingston-on-Thames, England. Later changed his name to what he considered its Anglo-Saxon form. **late 1840s:** Worked for his family's stationery business in London. **c. 1851:** Moved to New York. Worked as agent for British book publishers. Learned photography from a daguerreotypist. **1855:** Moved to San Francisco. Opened a bookstore specializing in illustrated books. Began photographing the life and architecture of San Francisco and its surroundings. **1860:** Was badly injured in a stagecoach accident. Went to England for treatment and recuperation. Studied photography. **c. 1865:** Returned to San Francisco and resumed his photographic documentation of the city in earnest. **1867:** First photographed in Yosemite. Signed his photographs "Helios," written in Greek. **1868:** Photographed for the U.S. government in the newly acquired territory of Alaska. **1869–71:** Free-lance photography for the U.S. government along the northern Pacific coast. **1872:** Returned to Yosemite to make an extensive series of mammoth-plate views. As a result of this series, was acclaimed foremost photographer of western landscape. Hired by Leland Stanford to analyze movements of a running horse. **1874:** Killed his wife's lover. Court ruled that the homicide was justifiable. Muybridge was acquitted. **1875:** Traveled and photographed in Central America. **1876:** Resumed experiments for Stanford. **1878:** Published first sequence of photographs of a running horse. **1880:** Projected sequential photographs onto a screen in rapid succession—the first "movies." **1881:** Traveled in Europe. Widely honored for his motion studies. **1883–85:** At the University of Pennsylvania in Philadelphia, made extensive series of sequential photographs of human and animal motion. **1887:** Published 781 of his motion studies in the eleven volumes of *Animal Locomotion.* Subscribers to the publication included many of the most important American and European artists and scientists. **c. 1896:** Returned to England. **1904:** Died in Kingston-on-Thames.

Nadar

page 43

1820: Born Gaspard-Félix Tournachon in Paris. **1838:** Family moved to Lyons. Began to study medicine and to write drama criticism for local newspapers. **1839:** Returned to Paris. Wrote drama criticism for Parisian publications. **1840–45:** Various journalistic and literary projects. Became prominent in bohemian literary and artistic circles. **c. 1845:** Began drawing caricatures for popular press. Became one of the foremost caricaturists of the time. **1854:** Published huge lithograph entitled *Le Panthéon Nadar,* brilliantly caricaturing some three hundred contemporary French writers. It was a great success. Opened first photographic studio and began to make portraits—primarily of his many friends among the literary, artistic, and radical political elite. **1858:** After several unsuccessful attempts, made the world's first aerial photographs—views of Paris taken from a balloon. Three years earlier he had patented the idea of using aerial photographs for surveying and military reconnaissance. **1860:** Stopped making salt prints and began to make albumen prints from wet-collodion negatives. Experimented with electric lighting for making exposures and printing. In the margin of the photograph of Monsieur D's hand, Nadar wrote, "Negative made with daylight. Print made by electric light." **1861:** Made the world's first underground photographs—views of the Paris sewers and catacombs illuminated with carbon arc lamps connected to Bunsen batteries in the streets above. **1870:** Organized balloon corps to break the Siege of Paris. Carried the world's first airmail from Paris to Normandy. Period of greatest portraits came to an end. **1874:** Lent his studio to the Impressionists for their first group exhibition. **1886:** Conducted the world's first photo-interview, with Michel-Eugène Chevreul (1786–1889), a famous chemist whose color theories were at the time greatly influencing the work of Seurat and the other Neo-Impressionist painters. Nadar interviewed Chevreul, who was then one hundred years old, while his son Paul Nadar operated the camera. **1887:** When his wife suffered a stroke, Nadar gave up his photographic studio and moved with her to a country house south of Paris. Remained there until 1896. Paul Nadar took over the Paris studio. **1897:** Opened a photographic studio in Marseilles. **1904:** Returned to Paris. Wrote his memoirs. **1910:** Died in Paris.

Nègre, Charles

pages 45, 48

1820: Born in Grasse, France. **c. 1839:** Began studies with the academic history painter Paul Delaroche in Paris. **1843:** Left Delaroche's studio. Studied briefly with Ingres. First exhibited a painting in the Salon. **c. 1844:** Began making daguerreotypes of his paintings. **c. 1849:** Began making photographs with salted paper processes. **1851:** Designed a lens that enabled him to photograph with exposure times short enough to record moving people. One of the first photographers to focus on everyday life (genre scenes). Made numerous photographs in the streets and markets of Paris. Photographed the town and cathedral of Chartres. **1852:** Taught drawing at the Ecole Superieure du Commerce in Paris. Beginning in August, photographed extensively in the south of France. Took about two hundred photographs for album *Le Midi de la France.* **1854:** Began publication of *Le Midi de la France,* which he never completed. Began experiments to develop a photogravure process. **1855-61:** Many photographic awards and commissions, including, in 1859, an important series on the Imperial Asylum at Vincennes. **1861:** Forced by ill health to retire to Nice. **1862-78:** Continued to photograph and to exhibit and publish his work. Developed an accurate but impractical photogravure process. **1880:** Died in Grasse.

O'Sullivan, Timothy H.

page 62

c. 1840: Born in New York. **c. 1855:** Apprenticed to Mathew Brady. Worked first in Brady's New York gallery, then transferred to his Washington studio, which was managed by Alexander Gardner. **1861:** Began to photograph the Civil War for Brady. At Bull Run, his camera was hit by a Confederate shell. **1862:** With Gardner and others who protested against Brady's failure to give credit to his photographers, resigned from Brady's staff. Hired by Gardner to continue photographing the Civil War. **1864:** Photographed the aftermath of the Battle of Gettysburg. **1865:** Helped Gardner make prints for *Gardner's Photographic Sketch Book of the War.* Forty-four out of one hundred images in the book signed by O'Sullivan. **1867:** Hired by Clarence King as photographer for his survey of the land along the fortieth parallel of latitude between Denver and Virginia City, Nevada. The survey was to study all aspects of the terrain along the proposed route of the Central Pacific Railroad. **1868:** Photographed with magnesium flash in mines in Virginia City. **1869:** At conclusion of the King survey, returned to New York. **1870:** Photographed on survey of possible routes for Panama Canal. **1871:** Photographed in Nevada, Utah, Arizona, and New Mexico for Lt. George M. Wheeler's Geological Surveys West of the 100th Meridian. **1872:** Photographed with Clarence King along Central Pacific Railroad in Utah. **1873:** Returned to Wheeler survey. Photographed in Arizona, including Canyon de Chelly. **1875:** When Wheeler survey was completed, settled in Baltimore. Made prints for Wheeler survey albums. **1880:** Appointed chief photographer for U.S. Treasury Department. **1882:** Died of tuberculosis in Washington, D.C.

Primoli, Count Giuseppe

page 66

1851: Born in Rome. Mother was Napoleon's grandniece. **1852:** Louis Napoleon became Emperor Napoleon III of France. **1853-70:** Family lived in Paris and moved in the highest circles of the court. **1870:** At the outbreak of the Franco-Prussian War, family returned to Rome. **1870s-1880s:** Visited many of the royal courts of Europe. Spent much time in Paris, where he made many friends among the most important writers, artists, musicians, actors, and actresses. **late 1880s:** Took up photography. **1890s-early 1900s:** Continued to travel and to photograph, decreasing activity as family fortune dwindled. **1927:** Died in Rome.

Ray, Man *see* Man Ray

Regnault, Victor

page 41

1810: Born in Aix-la-Chapelle, France. **1825:** While working as a clerk in a Parisian fancy-goods store, studied mathematics independently at the Bibliothèque Nationale. **1830-32:** Studied at the Ecole Polytechnique. **1832-34:** Studied at the Ecole des Mines. **1836:** Appointed professor of chemistry at the Ecole Polytechnique. **1840:** Elected to the Académie des Sciences. **1845-46:** Began photographing. **1847:** Aided Blanquart-Evrard in his efforts to improve Talbot's calotype process. **1851:** Became a founding member of the Société Héliographique. **1851-55:** Gave negatives to Blanquart-Evrard for printing and publication. **1852-71:** Director of the state porcelain factory at Sèvres. **1854-68:** First president of the Société Française de Photographie. **1878:** Died in Paris.

Riis, Jacob

page 59

1849: Born in Ribe, Denmark. **1866-70:** Apprenticed to a carpenter in Copenhagen. **1870:** Immigrated to the United States. It was a period of economic depression, and Riis could not find work. Lived in abject poverty in New York City. **1873:** Got a job with a news bureau in New York. **1877:** Became a police reporter for the New York *Tribune* and the Associated Press. Spent much time in the slums on the Lower East Side. **1884:** Instrumental in the formation of the Tenement House Commission. **1888-90:** Left the *Tribune* for the *Evening Sun.* Wrote *How the Other Half Lives.* At first assisted by two amateur photographers, Henry G. Piffard and Richard Hoe Lawrence, but soon learned photography himself. One of the first photographers in the United States to use flash powder, which had been invented in Germany in 1887. Flash powder enabled Riis to photograph inside dark tenements and at night. **1890s-1910s:** Wrote many books about slums and the poor. Lectured extensively. **1914:** Died in Barre, Massachusetts.

Rodchenko, Alexander

pages 106, 110, 120, 126, 134

1891: Born in St. Petersburg, Russia. **c. 1902:** Family moved to Kazan. **1910-14:** Studied at the Kazan Art School. **1914:** Studied at the Stroganov Institute, Moscow. **1915:** Began making abstract drawings with a compass and a ruler. Met the abstract painter Kazimir Malevich. **1916:** Participated in Vladimir Tatlin's exhibition, *The Store.* **1917:** Worked with Tatlin and others on decoration for interior of Café Pittoresque, Moscow. **1918:** Following the Russian Revolution, was very active in the government agencies responsible for reorganizing art schools and museums throughout the Soviet Union. Began making wooden "Spatial Constructions." **1920-30:** Taught at the Higher State Art-Technical Studios (Vkhutemas/Vkhutein). **1921:** Stopped painting and began to work in typography and in design for textiles and porcelain. **1922:** Worked with director

Dziga Vertov on newsreels. **1923:** Began working with poet Vladimir Mayakovsky on advertisements and posters. Made his first photomontages to illustrate Mayakovsky's poem "About This." Graphic designer for periodical *Lef,* edited by Mayakovsky. **1923-24:** Having started to make photographs to use in his photomontages, became interested in photography as an artistic and communicational medium. **1924:** Began working as a photojournalist. Photographs published in *Lef* and other periodicals. **1925:** Went to Paris to supervise construction of workers' clubroom he had designed for the Soviet pavilion at the Exposition Internationale des Arts Décoratifs. **1928-29:** Contributed photographs and typographic design to magazine *Novyi Lef* (New Left Front of the Arts). **1928:** Joined the artists' group *October.* **1931:** Expelled from *October* for formalism. **1930s:** Worked as a photojournalist, specializing in coverage of sports and construction work. **1940s:** Organized photographic exhibitions and designed posters and commemorative albums for the Soviet government. Returned to abstract painting. **1956:** Died in Moscow.

Shahn, Ben   *pages 83, 85, 121, 140, 142*

1898: Born in Kovno (Kaunas), Lithuania. **1906:** Family immigrated to United States. Settled in Brooklyn, New York. **1911:** Apprenticed to a lithographer. Went to school at night. **1917-19:** Attended New York University. Won summer scholarships to study biology at the Marine Biological Laboratory, Woods Hole, Massachusetts. Paid for education by continuing to work part time as a lithographer. **1919-20:** Attended City College of New York. **1920:** Left college to study at the National Academy of Design and the Art Students League, New York. **1925:** First trip to Europe. Lived in Paris. Traveled in Italy, Austria, Netherlands, Spain, and North Africa. **1926:** Returned to the United States. Painted in New York and Truro, Massachusetts. **1927:** Returned to Paris to paint. **1929:** Returned to New York. Began to share studio with Walker Evans. **1931:** Worked on a series of paintings dealing with the Sacco and Vanzetti murder case. **1933:** Worked with Mexican painter Diego Rivera on mural for RCA Building, Rockefeller Center, New York. With minimal instruction from Evans, began making photographs of New York street scenes. **1934:** Worked on murals for Rikers Island Penitentiary. **1935:** Hired by the Special Skills section of the Resettlement Administration. During the fall, was "loaned" to the Historical Section of the RA to photograph throughout the Southeast. Made some six thousand photographs in about three months. **1936:** Began to make paintings based on RA photographs. **1937:** Photographed for the RA in Pennsylvania mining towns. **1938:** Photographed for the Farm Security Administration in Ohio. Thereafter, virtually stopped making photographs. **1939-69:** Received great acclaim as a painter, illustrator, and graphic artist. **1969:** Died in Roosevelt, New Jersey.

Sheeler, Charles   *pages 101, 112*

1883: Born in Philadelphia. **1900-3:** Studied applied design at the Philadelphia School of Industrial Art. **1903-6:** Attended the Pennsylvania Academy of the Fine Arts, where he studied painting with William Merritt Chase. **1912:** Decided on architectural photography as a means of supporting himself while he painted. **1913:** Exhibited six paintings in the Armory Show in New York. **1914:** Began to base his paintings on his photographs. Met Alfred Stieglitz. Gave up architectural photogra-

phy for photographic copying of works of art. **1919:** Moved to New York. Met Paul Strand. **c. 1920:** Began making photographs of New York from high viewpoints, looking down onto the roofs of lower buildings. **1921:** Collaborated with Strand on film *Mannahatta.* **early 1920s:** Worked at Marius de Zayas's Modern Gallery. **1923:** Hired by Steichen to do fashion and portrait photography for Condé Nast Publications—*Vogue* and *Vanity Fair.* Also free-lance advertising work. Most important client was N. W. Ayer and Son of Philadelphia. **1927:** Photographed the Ford Motor Company plant at River Rouge, Michigan. The photographs, which were widely published, brought him international fame as a photographer. **1928:** Began painting industrial subjects. **1929:** Resigned from Condé Nast. Traveled to Europe to see Deutsche Werkbund exhibition *Film und Foto,* in which he was represented. Photographed in Chartres. **1932:** Discontinued free-lance advertising photography. From this date on, concentrated on painting. **1935-36:** Photographed at Williamsburgh, Virginia, and executed paintings based on the photographs. **1939:** Major retrospective, which included photographs, at the Museum of Modern Art, New York. **1942-45:** Photographed works of art—especially Assyrian reliefs—for the Metropolitan Museum of Art, New York. **1950-51:** Photographed buildings in New York, including Rockefeller Center and the United Nations. **1965:** Died in Irvington, New York.

Southworth, Albert Sands and Josiah Johnson Hawes   *page 42*

1808: Hawes born in East Sudbury (now Wayland), Massachusetts. **1811:** Southworth born in West Fairlee, Vermont. **1820s:** While apprenticed to a carpenter, Hawes taught himself to paint portraits. **1829-41:** Hawes worked as an itinerant portrait painter. **1833-35:** Southworth attended Phillips Academy, Andover, Massachusetts. **1839:** Southworth opened a drugstore in Cabotville (now Chicopee), Massachusetts. **1840:** Southworth and Hawes, independently, attended a series of lectures in Boston about daguerreotypy. Southworth then went to New York to learn more from Joseph Pennell, his former roommate at Andover, who was assisting the painter Samuel F. B. Morse with his experiments in daguerreotypy and telegraphy. Southworth learned the daguerreian process from Morse, then returned to Cabotville with Pennell to open daguerreotype portrait studio. **1841:** Southworth and Pennell moved their studio to Boston. Hawes gave up painting and began making daguerreotypes. **1843:** Pennell retired. Hawes became Southworth's partner. **1849:** Southworth went to California in search of gold, but did not dissolve partnership with Hawes. Made daguerreotype views of San Francisco. **1851:** Southworth returned to Boston and resumed making daguerreotype portraits. Throughout the 1840s and 1850s, Southworth and Hawes were the greatest American daguerreotype portraitists. Like those of Nadar in France, their portraits were sensitive, direct, spontaneous, sympathetic, and uncluttered. Among their most distinguished sitters were Daniel Webster, Ralph Waldo Emerson, Harriet Beecher Stowe, and Lola Montez. **1862:** Partnership dissolved. **1894:** Southworth died. **1901:** Hawes died.

Steichen, Edward   *pages 71, 72, 78, 100, 122*

1879: Born in Luxembourg. **1881:** Family immigrated to United States. Settled in Hancock, Michigan. **1889:** Family moved to Milwaukee, Wisconsin. **1894-98:** Apprenticeship with American Fine Art Company, Milwaukee lithographic firm. Worked on advertising design. **1895:** Purchased his first camera. **1899:** Showed two photographs in the Second Philadelphia Photographic Salon. **1900:** Showed several photographs in Chicago Salon. The eminent Pictorialist Clarence H. White was so impressed by these photographs that he wrote Steichen a letter of encouragement. He also wrote to Stieglitz about Steichen, who visited New York later that year and met Stieglitz, who bought three photographs. Went to Paris. **1901:** Lived in Paris. Photographed artists and writers. Met Rodin. Painted as well as photographed. **1902:** Returned to New York. Rented a studio at 291 Fifth Avenue. With Stieglitz and others, founded the Photo-Secession. **1903:** Stieglitz published twelve photographs by Steichen in *Camera Work*. **1904:** Began to experiment with color photography. **1905:** With Stieglitz, organized the Little Galleries of the Photo-Secession in his former studio at 291 Fifth Avenue. **1906-14:** Lived in France. **1907:** Worked with Lumière Autochrome (color) plates. Ten of his color photographs exhibited at "291." **1908:** Photographed Rodin's monument to Balzac. **1910:** Arranged show of Cézanne watercolors at "291." **1911:** Began fashion photography. Continued to paint. **1913:** Double issue of *Camera Work* devoted to Steichen. **1914:** Returned to New York. Worked with Stieglitz at "291." **1917-19:** Served as an officer in the United States Army in France. Developed aerial reconnaissance photography. **1920:** Gave up painting in favor of photography. **1921:** Photographed Isadora Duncan and her students on the Acropolis in Athens. **1923:** Returned to New York. Was hired as chief photographer for Condé Nast Publications. Began fashion and portrait photography for *Vogue* and *Vanity Fair*. **1923-37:** Great artistic and financial success as fashion, portrait, and advertising photographer. **1929:** With Edward Weston, organized American section of Deutsche Werkbund exhibition *Film und Foto*, Stuttgart. **1938:** Retired from commercial work. **1942-45:** Director of United States Navy Photographic Institute. In charge of all navy combat photography. **1947:** Appointed director of the Department of Photography at the Museum of Modern Art, New York. **1952-55:** Prepared the photographic exhibition *The Family of Man*. **1962:** Resigned from MoMA. **1973:** Died in West Redding, Connecticut.

Steiner, Ralph

pages 92, 94

1899: Born in Cleveland, Ohio. **c. 1916:** Bought a simple camera and began photographing. **1917-21:** Attended Dartmouth College, Hanover, New Hampshire. Became seriously interested in photography. **1921-22:** Attended the Clarence H. White School of Photography in New York. **1922:** Got a job in a photogravure plant, where he made the plates for Robert Flaherty's portfolios of photographs of Eskimos. **1923:** Left photogravure plant and began working as an advertising and magazine photographer. Began making sharp-focus photographs of New York with a four- by five-inch Korona camera. Many of these early photographs include signs, and many have a humorous edge. **c. 1927:** Met Paul Strand and was greatly impressed by his mastery of technique. **1928:** Influenced by Strand, bought an eight- by ten-inch camera. Photographed in and around Saratoga Springs, New York. **1929:** Showed ten photographs in Deutsche Werkbund exhibition *Film und Foto*, Stuttgart. Made a short film, entitled H_2O, of the patterns of light reflections of water. **1930:** Portfolio of his personal—as opposed to commercial—photographs published in *Fortune*. **early 1930s:** Continued to make experimental films. **1935:** Worked with Strand and Leo Hurwitz as a cameraman for *The Plow That Broke the Plains*, a documentary film about the dust bowl. The film was produced by the Resettlement Administration and directed by film critic Pare Lorentz. **1938:** Collaborated with photographer Willard Van Dyke on *The City*, a humorous film dealing with the need for city planning. **1939:** *The City* was shown continuously at the New York World's Fair, where it was a tremendous success. **late 1930s-early 1940s:** Worked as picture editor for weekly newspaper *PM*. **late 1940s:** Spent four years in Hollywood working as a writer and an assistant director. **c. 1950:** Returned to New York, where Walker Evans hired him to photograph business executives for *Fortune*. **1950s-1970s:** Continued to do commercial and personal photography and to make films. Lives and works in Vermont.

Stieglitz, Alfred

page 70

1864: Born in Hoboken, New Jersey. **1871:** Family moved to Manhattan. **1879-81:** Attended City College of New York. **1881:** Studied at Realgymnasium, Karlsruhe, Germany. **1882:** Began to study mechanical engineering at Berlin Polytechnic. **1883:** Bought his first camera and enrolled in a photography course at the Berlin Polytechnic. Abandoned mechanical engineering in favor of photochemistry. **late 1880s:** Studied history and anthropology at the University of Berlin. Photographed in Germany, Switzerland, Austria, and Italy. **1887:** Was awarded first prize in a competition judged by the great English naturalistic photographer Peter Henry Emerson. **1890:** Returned to New York. **1893:** Became editor of *American Amateur Photographer*. **1897:** Became editor of *Camera Notes*, the magazine of the New York Camera Club. **1902:** Resigned as editor of *Camera Notes*. Founded the Photo-Secession, a group devoted to the advancement of photography as art. **1903:** Published first issue of *Camera Work*. **1905:** With Edward Steichen, founded the Little Galleries of the Photo-Secession, known as "291" from its address, 291 Fifth Avenue. **1908-17:** Exhibitions at "291" included, in addition to photography, works by such artists as Picasso, Matisse, Rodin, Cézanne, Brancusi, John Marin, Marsden Hartley, and Georgia O'Keeffe, as well as several pioneering shows of children's art. **1910:** Organized the International Exhibition of Pictorial Photography at the Albright Art Gallery, Buffalo, New York. **c. 1911:** Began to turn from Pictorial to "straight" photography. **1915-16:** Published *291*, a magazine of the arts. **1917:** "291" closed. *Camera Work* ceased publication. Began series of photographs of Georgia O'Keeffe that extended to 1937. **c. 1920:** Began extensive series of cloud studies, called *Equivalents*. Continued through mid-1930s. **1924:** Married Georgia O'Keeffe. **1925:** Opened the Intimate Gallery, where he showed work by O'Keeffe, Marin, Hartley, Arthur Dove, Charles Demuth, and others. The only photographs exhibited there were by Paul Strand. **1929:** Closed The Intimate Gallery and founded An American Place. **1930s:** Series of New York views. Many photographs of trees and landscape around his summer home at Lake George, New York. Continued to mount varied exhibitions—including work by several photographers—at An American Place. **1937:** On account of illness, virtually stopped making and printing photographs. **1940-46:** Showed work by almost nobody except O'Keeffe, Marin, and Dove at An American Place. **1946:** Died in New York.

Strand, Paul
pages 80, 119, 137

1890: Born in New York City. **1907:** Began studying at Ethical Culture School in New York. Among his teachers was Lewis Hine, who took his class to see a major survey of Pictorialist photography at Alfred Stieglitz's "291" gallery. Hine introduced Stieglitz to the class. Strand decided to become a photographer. **1909:** Graduated from Ethical Culture School. **1912:** Went into business as a commercial photographer. **1913:** Strand's soft-focus Pictorialist style gradually changed by exposure to modern French art at "291" and the Armory Show. **1915:** Showed his bold new work to Stieglitz, who immediately promised to exhibit it and publish it in his influential magazine *Camera Work*. **1916:** Exhibition at "291." Several photographs in *Camera Work*. **1917:** The final issue of *Camera Work* was entirely devoted to Strand's photographs. **1921:** Collaborated with Charles Sheeler on film *Mannahatta*. **1926:** Photographed in New Mexico and Colorado. **1927-29:** Photographed in Maine and the Gaspé Peninsula. **1930-32:** Photographed in New Mexico during summers. **1932-34:** Photographed in Mexico. **1935:** Worked with Ralph Steiner and Leo Hurwitz on Pare Lorentz's film *The Plow That Broke the Plains* for the Resettlement Administration. **1937-43:** Worked on films. **1943-44:** Returned to still photography. Photographed in Vermont. **1946-47:** Worked with Nancy Newhall on book *Time in New England*. **1951:** Moved to France. **1952-53:** Photographed in Italy. **1954:** Photographed in the Outer Hebrides. **1955-57:** Photographed French artists and writers. **1959:** Photographed in Egypt. **1962:** Photographed in Morocco. **1963-64:** Photographed in Ghana. **1976:** Died in Orgeval, France.

Talbot, William Henry Fox
page 40

1800: Born in Melbury, Dorset, England. **1818-21:** Studied at Trinity College, Cambridge. **1822:** Elected a member of the Royal Astronomical Society. **1827:** Moved to Lacock Abbey, the house in Wiltshire that had belonged to his ancestors since the sixteenth century. **1832:** Became a Fellow of the Royal Society, the most august organization of British scientists. Elected to Parliament. **1833-34:** Served in the House of Commons. **1833:** While on vacation at Lake Como, Italy, tried to sketch the landscape and became extremely frustrated. Decided to experiment with imprinting images from a camera obscura directly and permanently on sensitized paper. **1834:** Made first "photogenic drawings" by placing small objects—such as leaves and pieces of lace—directly on sheets of paper sensitized with silver chloride and exposing them to light. The covered areas produced white silhouettes on a black background. The image appeared during exposure, without needing to be developed chemically. **1835:** During summer, made first successful negatives with a camera obscura. Conceived idea of making positives from negatives. **1835-38:** Photographed his family, Lacock Abbey, its staff, and its grounds. Published papers on mathematics and crystallography and a book on classical literature. **1839:** Daguerre's invention announced in Paris on January 7. Later that month, Talbot showed examples of his photographs at the Royal Society and published details of his process. **1840:** Invented the calotype process, in which the exposure in the camera produces a latent image that must be developed chemically. This process allowed exposure times much shorter than those needed for photogenic drawings. Talbot continued to photograph extensively. **1841:** Took out a patent on the calotype process. **1844-46:** Published *The Pencil of Nature*, containing twenty-four of his photographs, including views of Lacock Abbey, Oxford, and Paris as well as photogenic drawings and photographs of sculpture, of a drawing, and of a page from an old book (the ancestor of today's quick photo-copies). The photographs were intended to show photography's range. The book was illustrated with original prints that were tipped in, not engraved reproductions. **1851:** Took out a general patent on photography. Made first stop-action photographs with flash from electric spark. **1854:** Claimed that a London professional photographer violated terms of patent by making portraits with the wet-collodion process without having obtained a license from Talbot. Court ruled that although Talbot had invented negative/positive process, his patent covered only calotype process. **1854-77:** Did very little photographic work. Numerous scientific papers, translations of Assyrian inscriptions, and other writings. **1877:** Died at Lacock Abbey.

Thomson, John
page 64

1837: Born in Edinburgh, Scotland. **late 1850s:** Studied chemistry at the University of Edinburgh. **early 1860s:** Took up photography. **1862:** Traveled and photographed in Ceylon. **c. 1864:** Photographed architecture in Scotland. **1865-early 1870s:** Traveled and photographed extensively in the Far East. Sent photographs to Edinburgh and London for publication. **1867:** Published *The Antiquities of Cambodia*. **1869:** Published *The Visit of His Royal Highness, The Duke of Edinburgh, to Hong Kong in 1869*. **1870:** Published *Views of the North River*. **1872:** Published *Foo Chow and the River Min*. **1873-74:** Published *Illustrations of China and Its People*. **c. 1875-76:** Photographed the street tradespeople of London. **1877-78:** Published *Street Life in London*. **1878-79:** Traveled and photographed in Cyprus. **c. 1880:** Opened a portrait studio in London. **1880s-1890s:** Wrote extensively about photography. **1921:** Died in London.

Umbo
page 111

1902: Born Otto Umbehr in Dusseldorf. **1920:** Worked in a coal mine near Essen. **1921-23:** Studied design and metalwork at the Bauhaus, Weimar. **1923:** Moved to Berlin. Studied art. **1924-27:** Worked at various odd jobs, including house painter and clown. Made movie posters. Worked as a camera assistant on Walter Ruttmann's documentary film *Berlin: The Symphomy of a Great City*. Collaborated with Sasha Stone on photomontages for various publications. **1928:** Was a co-founder of the Dephot photographic agency. **1928-43:** Extensive photojournalism. **1943-45:** Served in the German Army. **1945-1970s:** Resumed photojournalism and advertising photography. **1957-74:** Taught photography in various schools. **1980:** Died in Germany.

Vachon, John
page 147

1914: Born in St. Paul, Minnesota. **1936:** Was hired as messenger and file clerk for Historical Section of federal Resettlement Administration. **1937:** Through contact with RA photographers and their work, became interested in making photographs himself. When RA became the Farm Security Administration, began photographing for FSA in Washington, D.C. **1938:** Began traveling for FSA. Photographed in Delaware, North Carolina, Georgia, Kansas, and Nebraska. **1939:**

Worked in the FSA office in Washington. **1939–40:** Photographed in North and South Dakota during the winter. **1941–42:** Traveled and photographed throughout the United States for the FSA. **1942:** When the Historical Section of the FSA was transferred to the Office of War Information, stayed with the section for a few months. **1943–45:** Served in the United States Army. **1945–75:** Free-lance photographer. **1973:** Was awarded John Simon Guggenheim Memorial Fellowship. **1973–74:** Photographed in North Dakota during the winter. **1975:** Died in New York City.

Watkins, Carleton

1829: Born in Oneonta, New York. **c. 1852:** Went to California. Settled in Sacramento. Worked as a carpenter. **1853:** Moved to San Francisco. Began working as a clerk in a department store. **1854:** Was hired as a temporary clerk in the daguerreotype studio of Robert H. Vance in San Francisco. Quickly learned daguerreotypy and was hired permanently. **late 1850s:** Vance studio switched to the wet-collodion process. **1861:** Made extensive series of stereographs and mammoth-plate photographs in Yosemite. Was the first American landscape photographer to work with a mammoth-plate camera, which he had specially constructed for him. **1862–65:** Made several trips to photograph in Yosemite. **1866:** Photographed in Yosemite for the Josiah D. Whitney survey. The expedition party included Clarence King, who began his own survey the following year. **1867:** The San Francisco photographic dealer Thomas Houseworth entered Yosemite photographs by Watkins and others in Paris International Exposition under his own name. Won bronze medal. Watkins then copyrighted his Yosemite views. Opened his Yosemite Art Gallery in San Francisco. Became widely recognized as greatest American landscape photographer. **1868:** Photographed Pacific coast from San Francisco to Oregon and photographed extensively in Oregon. **1870:** Photographed ascents of Mounts Lassen and Shasta for Clarence King survey. **1873:** Photographed along route of Central Pacific Railroad between San Francisco and Salt Lake City. **1873–74:** Went bankrupt in the financial panic. Lost all of his negatives and prints to his creditors, including I. W. Taber, who began to publish Watkins's Yosemite views under his own name. **1875–80:** Returned to Yosemite to duplicate his lost negatives. **c. 1880:** Began to concentrate on a series of tree "portraits" that he had started earlier. **1880s:** Photographed California landscapes, ranches, hotels, etc. Photographed everyday life in San Francisco. Sold photographs to tourists. **c. 1890:** Eyesight began to fail. **1906:** Had become blind. Was arranging for sale of his negatives and a complete set of prints to Stanford University when the fire following the San Francisco earthquake destroyed his studio and its contents. **1916:** Died in San Francisco.

Weegee

1899: Born Arthur Felling in Zloczew, Poland. **1909:** Family immigrated to the United States. Lived in poverty on Lower East Side, New York. **c. 1911–13:** Left school. Began working at a series of odd jobs, including street photographer. **1923–35:** Worked in the darkroom of Acme News Services. **1935:** Quit his job and became a free-lance photographer. Soon bought a car and equipped it with a police radio. Drove around high-crime areas of New York waiting for a bulletin to come over the radio. Would often reach the scene of a crime before the police. **1936–46:** Free-lance photography for New York newspapers and photo-syndicates. Specialized in coverage of violent crimes. Also fires and other disasters. Made many photographs at night with harsh flash. **1945:** Began using infrared film to photograph in the dark. **1946:** *Naked City*, a book of Weegee's sensationalistic news photographs, published. **1947:** Sold rights for a movie based on *Naked City*. **1947–55:** Lived in Hollywood. Worked as a photographic consultant for movies and as a bit actor. **1950s:** Began to specialize in trick photographs—grotesquely distorted portraits, kaleidoscopic and mirror images, stunts—made with special lenses, some of which Weegee designed himself. **1960s:** Continued trick photographs, especially portraits of actors and politicians and photographs of famous buildings. Made publicity photographs. Lectured throughout the United States. **1968:** Died in New York.

Weston, Edward

1886: Born in Highland Park, Illinois. **1902:** Received a camera from his father. **1903–6:** Worked for Marshall Field & Company in Chicago. Photographed in spare time. **1906:** Went to California for vacation and decided to remain. Worked as door-to-door portrait photographer. **1908–11:** Attended Illinois College of Photography. Spent summers in California, working in photographic studios. **1911:** Opened portrait studio in Tropico (now Glendale), California. Became successful portraitist in soft-focus style. **1920:** Began to explore artistic potential of photography. **1922:** Traveled to New York. Photographed Armco steel mill in Middleton, Ohio, on the way. In New York, met Alfred Stieglitz, Paul Strand, and Charles Sheeler. **1923:** Moved to Mexico City with Tina Modotti. **1924:** Stopped using his soft-focus lenses. Bought a cheap Rapid-Rectilinear lens whose tiny aperture gave great depth of focus. Began studies of natural forms. **1925:** Returned to California for six months. **1926:** Returned to Mexico. Traveled and photographed extensively in Mexico. At the end of the year, returned to California. **1927:** Began classic work—close-ups of contorted nudes, peppers, shells, trees, etc. **1928:** Opened a portrait studio in San Francisco with his son, Brett. **1929:** Moved to Carmel. Began photographing natural forms on the beach and in the woods at nearby Point Lobos. With Edward Steichen, organized the American section of the Deutsche Werkbund exhibition *Film und Foto*, Stuttgart. **1932:** With Ansel Adams, Imogen Cunningham, Willard Van Dyke, and others, founded Group f.64 *(see Adams biography)*. *The Art of Edward Weston*, a book of thirty-nine photographs edited by Merle Armitage, was published. **1930s:** Continued nudes, close-ups of natural forms, and landscapes. **1937:** Became the first photographer to be awarded a John Simon Guggenheim Memorial Fellowship. Traveled and photographed extensively in the West and the Southwest. **1938:** Fellowship renewed. Married Charis Wilson. **1939:** Returned to Point Lobos. Photographed M.G.M. studios in Culver City, California. **1941:** Traveled in southern and eastern United States making photographs commissioned by Limited Editions Club for special edition of Walt Whitman's *Leaves of Grass*. **1942–45:** Civil defense work. Photographic satires. Became ill with Parkinson's disease. **1948:** Photographed at Point Lobos. Illness prevented further work. **1949–58:** Supervised his son, Brett, in printing his life's work. **1958:** Died in Carmel, California.

White, Minor
page 161

1908: Born in Minneapolis, Minnesota. **1920:** His grandfather gave him a projector and a collection of lantern slides, which stimulated his interest in photography. **1928–33:** Studied botany and English at the University of Minnesota. **1933–37:** Wrote poetry and worked at various jobs. **1937:** Began serious photography. Moved to Portland. Joined the Oregon Camera Club. Exhibited locally. **1938–41:** Photographed for the Works Progress Administration in Portland. Taught photography at the La Grande Art Center, a WPA center in eastern Oregon. **1941:** His photographs first shown at the Museum of Modern Art in New York (*Image of Freedom* group show). **1942–45:** Served in the United States Army. Did little photography. **1945:** Moved to New York City. Studied art history and aesthetics at the Columbia University Extension Division. **1946:** Met Alfred Stieglitz, Edward Steichen, and Paul Strand. Appointed to the photographic faculty of the San Francisco Institute of Fine Arts (now the San Francisco Art Institute) by Ansel Adams. Developed friendship with Adams. Visited Edward Weston at Point Lobos. **1949–52:** Photographed many plays in San Francisco. **1952:** With Adams, Beaumont and Nancy Newhall, Dorothea Lange, Barbara Morgan, and others founded *Aperture*, a quarterly journal of photography. **1953:** Appointed assistant curator (under Beaumont Newhall) at the George Eastman House in Rochester, New York. **1955:** Began teaching at the Rochester Institute of Technology. Became interested in mysticism and Zen Buddhism. **1956:** Resigned from Eastman House. Became very interested in Oriental life and philosophy. **1959:** Traveled across United States. Photographed extensively. **1960–75:** Continued as editor-publisher of *Aperture*. Gave many lectures and workshops. **1976:** Died.

Winogrand, Garry
page 165

1928: Born in New York. **1946–47:** Served eighteen months in the Army Air Force. Began photographing. **1947:** Studied painting at the City College of New York. **1948:** Transferred to Columbia University. Planned to study painting, but joined camera club and was soon committed to photography. **1952:** Began free-lance photojournalism. Photographs published in *Colliers*, *Pageant*, *Sports Illustrated*, and elsewhere. **1955:** Two photographs included in exhibition *The Family of Man* at the Museum of Modern Art, New York. Saw Walker Evans's book *American Photographs* and was deeply moved by it. Set out on a photographic trip across the United States. **late 1950s:** Abandoned photojournalism in favor of advertising photography. **early 1960s:** In his personal work, increasingly influenced by Robert Frank's book *The Americans*. **1963:** Began photographing in New York City zoos and at the Coney Island Aquarium. **1964:** Was awarded a John Simon Guggenheim Memorial Fellowship. Traveled and photographed in California and the Southwest. **1967:** Photographs shown with those of Diane Arbus and Lee Friedlander at the Museum of Modern Art. **1969:** Published *The Animals*, a book of his zoo photographs. Began teaching photography. Was awarded a second Guggenheim fellowship. **1969–73:** Photographed the "effect of the media on events." **mid-1970s–present:** Lives and works in Los Angeles.